Pan Study Aids
'O' Level/CSE/16+ Revision Cards

# Physics

J. J. Welling

Pan Books  London and Sydney

# Pan Study Aids 'O' level/CSE/16+ Revision Cards

## PREFACE

These notes are for **revision** only. They are not a replacement for a complete textbook, practical work or a teacher. All the laws, general principles and formulae needed for CSE, 16+ and O level are included. No detailed instructions for experimental work or practical proofs of laws are included. SI units are used throughout, a solidus being used with derived units, e.g. m/s (metres per second) instead of $ms^{-1}$. This style is used by almost every exam board.

### Hints for revision

**1  Do:**

- ★ check an up-to-date copy of the exam syllabus that you are following to see which topics you need to learn;
- ★ plan a revision timetable – take one topic at a time, using your syllabus as a checklist;
- ★ practise plenty of questions and problems, especially questions from past papers;
- ★ revise in a quiet room, using a reading lamp if possible;
- ★ revise with a pencil and rough paper in front of you to jot down notes and formulae and to sketch diagrams;
- ★ try to understand a definition or principle rather than learning it 'parrot fashion' – understanding helps you to remember.

**2  Don't:**

- ★ revise for a long stretch without a break – one hour is quite enough, then have a rest;
- ★ work late at night – brains become tired;
- ★ leave your revision until the night before the exam.

Finally, good luck with your exam.

# CONTENTS

# 1 GENERAL IDEAS IN PHYSICS

## Units and measurement

### *SI units*
The agreed system of units is the Système International – SI for short. The three most basic units are:
1 length – the **metre** (m);
2 mass – the **kilogram** (kg);
3 time – the **second** (s).
Other units are derived from these, e.g. speed (m/s), density ($kg/m^3$).

### *SI units used in O level/16+/CSE*

| Quantity | Unit used and symbol | |
|---|---|---|
| Mass | kilogram | kg |
| Length | metre | m |
| Time | second | s |
| Current | ampere | A |
| Temperature | kelvin | K |
| Force | newton | N |
| Energy ⎫<br>Work ⎭ | joule | J |
| Power | watt | W |
| Pressure | pascal | Pa |
| Frequency | hertz | Hz |
| Charge | coulomb | C |
| PD ⎫<br>EMF ⎭ | volt | V |
| Resistance | ohm | $\Omega$ |
| Velocity | | m/s |
| Acceleration | | $m/s^2$ |
| Momentum | | kg m/s |
| Density | | $kg/m^3$ |
| Expansivity | | /K (or /°C) |
| Specific heat capacity | | J/kg K |
| Specific latent heat | | J/kg |
| Resistivity | | $\Omega$ m |

| Quantity | Unit used and symbol | |
| --- | --- | --- |
| Commonly used non-SI units | | |
| Energy | kilowatt hour | kWh |
| Pressure | millimetre of mercury | mmHg |
| Temperature | degree Celsius | °C |
| Density | | g/cm$^3$ |

## Prefixes for SI units

| prefix | Symbol | Factor |
| --- | --- | --- |
| mega- | M | $10^6$ |
| kilo- | k | $10^3$ |
| centi- | c | $10^{-2}$ |
| milli- | m | $10^{-3}$ |
| micro- | µ | $10^{-6}$ |
| nano- | n | $10^{-9}$ |

## Density and its measurement

1 The density of a body is its mass divided by its volume:

$$\text{Density} = \frac{\text{Mass}}{\text{Volume}} \text{ in kg/m}^3$$

Different materials have different densities, e.g. lead = 11,400 kg/m$^3$, iron = 8,000 kg/m$^3$, water = 1,000 kg/m$^3$, air = 1.3 kg/m$^3$.

2 The density of a **solid** can be found by measuring its mass *and* its volume, then dividing mass by volume. Mass can be measured using a top-pan balance. Volume is found either:
  ★ for a **regular** shape, e.g. cube, cylinder, by measuring and calculating;
  ★ for an **irregular** shape by using a displacement method – object is immersed in water in a measuring cylinder, level of water goes up, difference between two readings shows the volume of the solid.

3 The density of a **liquid** can be found by either:
  ★ using a density bottle – a special bottle is filled with the liquid, the mass of liquid in the bottle being compared with the mass of the same volume of water:

$$\text{Relative density of liquid} = \frac{\text{Mass of liquid}}{\text{Mass of same volume of water}}$$

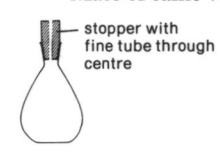

Fig. 1.1 *Density bottle*

★ if enough liquid is available a **hydrometer** can be floated in it – density can be read directly from the hydrometer scale (floats higher in dense liquids, lower in less dense ones).

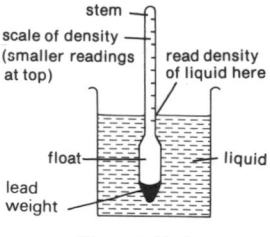

Fig. 1.2 *Hydrometer*

## The structure of matter

### Atoms and molecules

All substances are made up of **atoms**. An **element** contains atoms of only one kind – there are about 100 elements on earth. A **compound** contains at least two different elements joined together. Atoms join together in groups called **molecules,** e.g. a water molecule is formed from two hydrogen atoms and one oxygen atom.

### The kinetic theory

This states that all matter is made up of tiny particles (atoms or molecules). These particles:

1 are constantly moving, faster with higher temperature;
2 attract each other strongly when close to each other, repel each other if they come too close;
3 possess both kinetic and potential energy (see later).

### Brownian motion

Brownian motion is an indirect confirmation that molecules are constantly moving in every direction. Molecules are too small to be seen, but if they bombard very light particles which can be seen, the result of their motion may be detected. Smoke particles (about $10^{-6}$m) are introduced into an enclosed air cell. The particles are observed through a microscope and are seen as reflected silver dots randomly agitated (see Fig. 1.2). Brownian motion was first seen in a liquid as floating pollen grains agitated by water molecules.

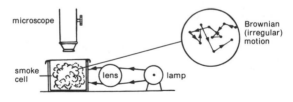

Fig. 1.3 *Observing Brownian Movement*

### Solids, liquids and gases

All matter exists in one of three states – **solids**, **liquids** and **gases**.

| Solids | Liquids | Gases |
|---|---|---|
| Particles in a closely packed regular arrangement | Particles in random motion, more closely packed than in a gas | Particles in random motion, at high speed |

| Solids | Liquids | Gases |
| --- | --- | --- |
| Particles vibrate about fixed position | Particles not held in fixed positions – free to change places with each other | Particles can move anywhere within the space available |
| No container needed – solids have a definite shape and volume | Definite volume, but no fixed shape | Gas particles exert a pressure on their container as they bombard it at high speed – no fixed volume or shape |

### Elasticity

1 Many solids, e.g. rubber, steel, return to their original size after they have been stretched *or* compressed (**elasticity**).

2 When an elastic material, e.g. a wire, a spring, has been stretched it returns to its original size due to **attractive** forces between molecules.

3 When an elastic material has been compressed, **repulsive** forces restore it to its original shape (when molecules are closer together than normal the forces between them are repulsive).

4 Materials are only elastic up to a certain point – beyond this they will not return to their original shape (**elastic limit**).

### Diffusion

Diffusion in liquids and gases provides further evidence that molecules have random motion.

1 Shown in **liquids** by placing a small copper sulphate crystal in a beaker of water. After a few days the undisturbed beaker contains a blue solution, denser than water, at the bottom of the beaker. After about a week the blue colour extends throughout the water due to constant movement of the molecules.

2 Movement of molecules in a **gas** shown by placing a gas jar containing air on top of a gas jar containing brown nitrogen dioxide. The brown gas is soon observed in the upper container.

**3** Diffusion in gases occurs faster than in liquids since gas molecules move more quickly and further between collisions.

**4** If naphthalene or camphor is left uncovered in a room, the camphor or naphthalene molecules diffuse into the air and can be smelt.

## Estimating the size of a molecule

The size of molecules varies, but 1 nm is typical. The size of an oil molecule can be roughly measured.

**1** A drop of olive oil is held in a fine wire loop. Its diameter is measured using a millimeter scale held behind it.

**2** Halve the diameter to give the radius ($r$) of the oil drop.

**3** Volume of oil = $\frac{4}{3}\pi r^3$.

**4** Lycopodium powder is sprinkled on clean level water surface.

**5** The oil drop is placed in the middle of the water. It quickly spreads across the surface, pushing back the powder.

**6** Diameter of oil film is measured, then halved to give radius ($R$).

**7** Area of oil film = $\pi R^2$.

**8** Thickness of oil film $= \dfrac{\text{Volume of oil}}{\text{Area of film}}$

$$= \frac{4/3\pi r^3}{\pi R^2}$$

**9** If the oil film is one molecule thick, this gives a rough value for the size of an oil molecule. If the film is two or more molecules thick the value gives an 'upper limit' to the size of a molecule.

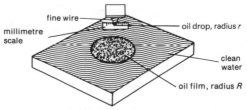

fine wire

millimetre scale

oil drop, radius $r$

clean water

oil film, radius $R$

Fig. 1.4 *Estimating the size of a molecule*

# 2 MECHANICS: FORCES AND MOTION

## Forces

A **force** changes a body's state of rest or of uniform motion in a straight line, i.e. it causes a body to start moving from rest *or* stops it when it is moving *or* causes it to change direction once it is moving.

### Mass, weight and gravity

1  The **mass** of an object (kg) is a measure of its inertia.
2  **Inertia** is resistance to change of motion.
3  The **weight** of a body is the pull of gravity on it. On the earth's surface a body's weight is less at the equator than at the poles since the earth's diameter is greater at the equator than at the poles – gravity varies with distance from the earth's centre (variation is usually small enough to be neglected). If the same body were weighed on the surface of the moon its weight would be less than on earth. Thus the mass of the planet influences weight.
4  The unit of force is the newton (N) – 1 newton is the force which produces an acceleration of $1 \, \text{m/s}^2$ when it acts on a mass of 1 kg.

### Gravitational field strength

Massive objects, e.g. the earth, the sun, are surrounded by a **gravitational field**. This exerts a pulling force on any mass in it. The size of this force depends on the **gravitational field strength**, e.g. near the earth's surface it is about 10 N/kg, so a mass of 1 kg has a weight of 10 newtons.

Weight = Mass × Gravitational field strength
$\qquad$ = 1 kg × 10 N/kg = 10 newtons

On earth, the gravitational field strength is $g$ (=9.81 N/kg). The moon's gravitational field strength is about 1.6 N/kg.

### Forces as vectors

1  A **vector** quantity has direction *and* magnitude, e.g. force.

**2** **Scalar** quantities have magnitude only.

| Scalar | Vector |
|--------|--------|
| Length | Force |
| Time | Velocity |
| Mass | Momentum |
| Pressure | Displacement |
| Density | |
| Speed | Acceleration |
| Energy | |
| Volume | |

### *Vector diagrams*

Vectors can be represented by a straight line in a vector diagram. Two vectors can be added by using the **parallelogram rule** (see Fig. 2.1) – if two or more forces act in different directions at a point on a body they will produce the same effect as a single or resultant force which can be determined by a vector diagram.

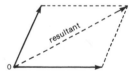

Fig. 2.1 *Parallelogram rule*

1  **Parallelogram of forces** – if two forces acting at a point are represented in magnitude and direction by the adjacent sides of a parallelogram, the resultant will be represented in magnitude and direction by the diagonal of the parallelogram drawn at this point.
2  **Triangle of forces** – if three forces acting on an object are in equilibrium they can be represented in magnitude and direction by the sides of a triangle taken in order (see Fig. 2.2).

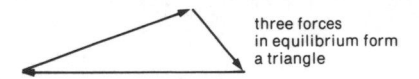

three forces
in equilibrium form
a triangle

Fig. 2.2 *Triangle of forces*

### Resolving a force into components

A single force can be replaced by two separate forces at right angles to each other (resolving a force into components – see Fig. 2.3). Other vectors, like velocity, can be resolved into two separate components, e.g. one horizontal, one vertical. These can be treated independently in calculations.

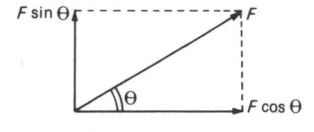

Fig. 2.3 *Resolving a force into its components*

## The turning effects of forces

### Moments

An applied force can exert a turning effect.

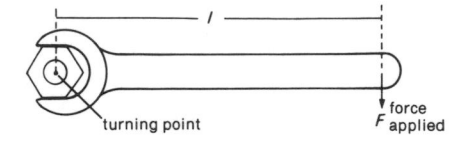

Fig. 2.4 *Moment of a force$=F\times l$ newton metres*

1  The **moment** of a force about a point is the product of the force and the perpendicular distance of its line of action from that point (measured in newton metres (Nm) – see Fig. 2.4).
2  **Principle of moments** – when a body is in equilibrium the sum of the clockwise moments at a point must equal the sum of the anticlockwise moments at that point.

**Example:** Fig. 2.5 shows a ruler balanced at O (fulcrum) and having two forces $F_1$ and $F_2$ acting on each side of the fulcrum.
$$F_2 \times d_2 = F_1 \times d_1$$

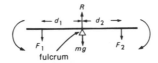

Fig. 2.5 *Balanced moments. Clockwise moments*$=F_2d_2$. *Anticlockwise moments*$=F_1d_1$. R$=F_1+$mg$+F_2$

3  A beam balance based on the principle of moments can be used to compare masses (any gravitational variations will equally affect both sides of the beam). The weight of the body whose mass is determined can be found by multiplying by $g$.

*Couples*
1  Two equal but *opposite* parallel forces together form a **couple**.
2  A couple gives rise to **angular** acceleration.

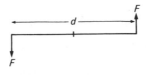

Fig. 2.6 *A couple. Moment*$=$Fd *newton metres*

3 Moment of a couple = Force × Perpendicular distance between forces.
4 The moment of a couple is often called a **torque**.

## Centre of mass

The centre of mass (**centre of gravity**) of a body is the single point through which its weight acts – the point of application of the resultant force due to any gravitational attraction on a body. The centre of gravity of:
1 a uniform rod or ruler is at its midpoint;
2 a uniform circular disc is at its centre;
3 a square, rectangle or regular block of constant material is at the crossing of its diagonals.

Note: the centre of gravity of a body need not be situated in the body itself, e.g. for a tripod or stool it is situated at a position in the air between the legs. The centre of gravity of a non-uniform or irregular object can be found.
1 A balancing method.
   * A flat irregular object is balanced on a straight edge and the balance line is traced using a pencil.
   * The object is turned to a different position and rebalanced.
   * The centre of gravity is where the two traced lines cross.
2 Using a plumb-line.
   * A plumb-line and irregular lamina are freely hung from the same point and the position of the string across the lamina is drawn when both are at rest.
   * This is repeated for different lamina positions.
   * The centre of gravity acts through the point where the lines cross.

## Equilibrium and stability

A body acted upon by two or more forces is in **equilibrium** if:
1 the sum of the moments of the forces taken about *any* point is zero;
2 the resultant force is zero.

A body is in:
1 **stable equilibrium** if it returns to its original position of rest after displacement (a small displacement raises its centre of gravity and gives rise to a restoring force);

16

2 **unstable equilibrium** if a small displacement lowers its centre of gravity and gives rise to a force increasing the displacement;
3 **neutral equilibrium** if a small displacement gives rise to zero resultant force (the height of its centre of gravity is not affected).

The stability of a body may be improved by lowering its centre of gravity or increasing the base area.

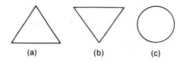

(a)  (b)  (c)

Fig. 2.7 *Equilibrium.* (*a*) *Stable.* (*b*) *Unstable.* (*c*) *Neutral*

**Forces on solids: elasticity**
Applied forces can stretch, compress or twist a material. A material's ability to return to its original shape is called **elasticity**.

*Hooke's law*
Providing the elastic limit is not exceeded, the deformation of a material is proportional to the force applied to it. Fig. 2.8 shows load applied plotted against extension produced, e.g. for a steel spring, elastic band, metal wire.

Fig. 2.8 *Hooke's law*

1   Providing the elastic limit has not been exceeded the material
    under investigation will retain its original form when the load
    is removed.
2   Beyond the elastic limit (A in Fig. 2.8) it is permanently
    distorted and never regains its original size or shape.
3   If further loading of the material takes place it eventually
    breaks (B).

To stretch, compress or twist a material requires forces which
distort the internal structure of that material. The work done to
produce extension of a wire or spring is the product of load and
extension.

## Forces in fluids

### Upthrust
A cork held under water or a balloon filled with hydrogen both
experience an upward force (**upthrust**). **Archimedes' principle** –
when a body is totally or partially immersed in a fluid (liquid or
gas) the upthrust on it is equal to the weight of fluid displaced,
verified by:
1   weighing an object in air;
2   re-weighing it in a liquid in a measuring cylinder;
3   the change in liquid level is observed;
4   the upthrust (difference in weights) is found to be the same as
    the weight of water displaced.

Any object released in a fluid will rise if the weight of a certain
volume of it is less than the weight of an equal volume of the
fluid. Similarly it will fall if the density of the object is greater
than that of the fluid. The **law of flotation** states that a floating
body displaces its own weight of the fluid in which it floats.

### Pressure due to a liquid
In Fig. 2.9:
1   Volume $= h \times A$;
2   Mass $= h \times \rho \times A$;

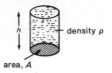

Fig. 2.9 *Pressure due to a liquid*

3  Weight = $h \times \rho \times g \times A$;
4  Pressure = $\dfrac{\text{Weight}}{\text{Area}}$ measured in N/m² (pascal).

5  Pressure due to liquid at depth $h = \dfrac{h\rho gA}{A}$
$$= h\rho g$$

where $\rho$ = density of the liquid.

Hydraulic machines use liquids under pressure. They use three important properties of liquids.
1  Liquids are almost **incompressible**.
2  When pressure is applied to a trapped liquid it is **transmitted** throughout the liquid.
3  The pressure in a liquid **acts in all directions**.

### Atmospheric pressure
**Atmospheric pressure** is due to the weight of the earth's atmosphere. A mercury **barometer** is used for measuring the

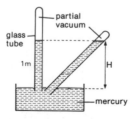

Fig. 2.10 *Mercury barometer*

pressure of the atmosphere. A glass tube about 1 m long and closed at one end is filled with mercury. It is carefully immersed under a trough of mercury, allowing no air to enter the system. On holding the inverted tube vertical the mercury level in the tube settles at a height of about 760 mm above that in the trough. Thus under normal conditions the pressure exerted by the atmosphere can support a mercury height of 760 mm.

1 The space above the mercury in the tube is almost a vacuum.
2 Tilting the tube does not affect the mercury height ($H$).

Pressure = Depth ($H$) × Density ($\rho$) × Gravity ($g$)

Thus atmospheric pressure is about 100,000 N/m$^2$ (or 100,000 Pa).

### The manometer

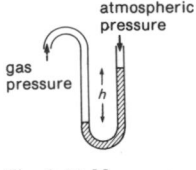

Fig. 2.11 *Manometer*

A **manometer** is used for measuring gas pressure differences. It consists of a U-tube half-filled with suitable liquid. If both ends of the tube are open to the atmosphere the liquid surfaces are at the same horizontal level since pressure on both is the same. A gas, of pressure to be measured, is introduced into one arm of the tube, forcing the liquid down on this side and up on the open side. When the excess pressure of the gas above atmospheric pressure is equal to the pressure due to the height of the liquid ($h$) the two are in equilibrium. Pressure below atmospheric pressure can be measured using a manometer; the liquid levels will be reversed so $h$ indicates the pressure difference below atmospheric pressure.

Note: if atmospheric pressure $P_o$ acts on the surface of a liquid, then at depth $h$:

Total pressure = $P_o + h\rho g$

## Motion

### *Speed and velocity*

1 **Speed** is the rate at which distance travelled by a body changes with time. It is a scalar quantity.

$$\text{Average speed} = \frac{\text{Total distance travelled}}{\text{Time taken}} \text{(m/s)}$$

2 **Displacement** is distance measured in a particular direction. **Velocity** is the rate at which displacement changes with time. Both displacement and velocity are vector quantities.

$$\text{Average velocity} = \frac{\text{Overall change in displacement}}{\text{Time taken}}$$

3 Uniform velocity occurs when the rate of change of displacement with time is constant.

### *Acceleration*

1 **Acceleration** is the rate at which velocity changes with time. It is a vector quantity.

$$\text{Average acceleration} = \frac{\text{Change in velocity}}{\text{Time taken}} \text{(m/s}^2\text{)}$$

2 Acceleration can be positive or negative (deceleration).
3 Uniform acceleration occurs when the velocity of a body changes by equal amounts in equal times.

### *Graphs showing motion*

1 **Distance–time** graphs (see Fig. 2.12) show the motion of a body. The gradient of a distance–time graph is the speed of the body.

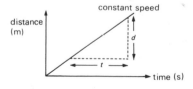

Fig. 2.12 *Distance–time graph. Speed=gradient=d/t*

21

2  **Velocity–time** graphs (see Fig. 2.13) show either uniform
velocity or uniform acceleration.
   * Gradient of velocity–time graph is acceleration:
   * Area underneath velocity–time graph is equal to distance
     moved.

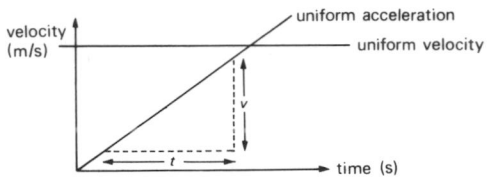

Fig. 2.13 *Velocity–time graph. Acceleration=gradient=v/t*

### Equations of motion

Most problems on motion can be solved using four equations:

1  $v = u + at$
2  $s = \frac{1}{2}(v + u)t$
3  $s = ut + \frac{1}{2}at^2$
4  $v^2 = u^2 + 2as$

Where $s$=displacement (m), $t$=time taken (s), $v$=final velocity
(m/s), $u$=initial velocity (m/s), $a$=acceleration (m/s$^2$).
Remember that $u$, $v$, $s$ and $a$ are vector quantities. For a
decelerating object $a$ is negative.

### Acceleration due to gravity

If there were no air resistance, all objects dropped near the earth
would accelerate towards the ground at the same rate, i.e.
acceleration due to gravity ($g$). It is roughly equal to 10 m/s$^2$. In a
laboratory $g$ can be measured (see Fig. 2.14).

1  A steel ball released from an electromagnetic support falls
   vertically due to gravity.
2  As the ball is released a centisecond timer is automatically
   started.

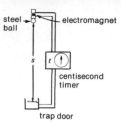

Fig. 2.14 *Measuring* g

3  The ball is allowed to strike a trap door after falling a
   measured distance ($s$).
4  As the trap door is broken the clock is stopped ($t$).
5  Using the equation $s = \frac{1}{2}at^2$

$$a = \frac{2s}{t^2}$$

   where $a = g$ and $s$ and $t$ are measured.
6  Hence $g$ can be calculated in $m/s^2$.

## Circular motion

Any object moving in a circle is being accelerated – it may be
travelling at a constant speed but its direction, and hence its
velocity, are continually changing. The force providing the
acceleration in circular motion is called **centripetal force**. It is
increased if:
1  the mass of the object is increased;
2  the radius of the circle is decreased;
3  the speed of the object increases.
The pull of gravity is the centripetal force which keeps a satellite
in orbit around the earth.

## Newton's laws of motion

### The three laws

1  Unless an external force acts on a body, its state of rest or
   uniform velocity in a straight line will not change. On earth it

is not possible to eliminate completely all the many forces that act on objects, making this law difficult to verify, although air pucks can be used to demonstrate it – they move fairly freely on a linear air track since there are practically no frictional forces between the two.

2 The momentum of a body is its mass $(m)\times$ its velocity $(v)$, i.e. momentum$=mv$. The rate of change of momentum of a body is proportional to the applied force and takes place in the direction of the applied force. Thus:

$$\text{Rate of change of momentum}=\frac{mv-mu}{t}$$

and as acceleration $(a)=\dfrac{v-u}{t}$:

$$F \propto ma$$

where $F$ is the force. Thus:

$$F=kma$$

where $k$ is a constant. By making the unit of force 1 N, producing an acceleration of $1\,\text{m/s}^2$ when acting on a mass of 1 kg, then:

$$F=ma, \text{ i.e. Force}=\text{Mass}\times\text{Acceleration}$$

3 To every action there is an equal and opposite reaction (the fundamental principle of rocket and jet engines).

### Conservation of momentum

**Law of conservation of momentum** – when bodies act on one another their total momentum remains constant providing no other external forces are involved. In any collision, total momentum *before* is equal to the total momentum *after* collision, e.g. two masses $m_1$ and $m_2$ collide:

$$m_1u_1+m_2u_2=m_1v_1+m_2v_2$$

where $u_1=$ initial velocity of $m_1$, $v_1=$ final velocity of $m_1$, $u_2=$ initial velocity of $m_2$, $v_2=$ final velocity of $m_2$.

## Work, energy and power

### Work
1 Work is a scalar quantity.

2 It is the product of the force applied and the distance moved by an object in the direction of the force.

3 Its unit is the joule (J).

1 J of work is done when a force of 1 N moves its point of application through 1 m in the direction of the applied force, i.e.:

$$1 J = 1 N \times 1 m$$

Work done (joules) = Force used (newtons) × Distance moved in direction of force (metres).

## Energy

Energy is the capacity to do work. The total **mechanical energy** of any object is equal to the sum of its potential energy and its kinetic energy.

1 **Potential energy** is energy by reason of position or state, e.g. water at high level, wound spring.
   * An object at a height above the ground has had work done to get it there.
   * Potential energy = $mgh$ joules
   where $m$ = mass of object, $h$ = height.

2 **Kinetic energy** is energy of motion, e.g. rotating flywheel, bullet in flight, falling stone.
   Kinetic energy = $\frac{1}{2}mv^2$ joules
   where $m$ = mass of object, $v$ = velocity.

## Conservation of energy

Energy exists in many different forms:

1 chemical energy, released by foods and fuels when they combine with oxygen;

2 electrical energy, provided by batteries and generators;

3 sound energy produced by vibrations;

4 radiant energy, e.g. from the sun, such as **light**;

5 nuclear energy released from the nuclei of some atoms;

6 thermal energy – the energy an object possesses because of the kinetic and potential energy of its molecules (often called **heat**).

Energy is often changed or converted from one form to another. The **law of conservation of energy** states that energy can neither be created nor destroyed, merely changed from one form to another (this is the most important law in physics).

### Power

Power is work done per second (measured in watts).

$$\text{Power} = \frac{\text{Work done (joules)}}{\text{Time taken (seconds)}}$$

$$= \frac{\text{Energy converted (J)}}{\text{Time taken (s)}}$$

Electrical power is often measured in kilowatts (kW).

## Machines and friction

Levers, pulleys and ramps are simple machines. In most machines an effort is applied by an energy source, e.g. a human, to lift a load. Usually effort and load are not equal.

### *Mechanical advantage (MA)*

Ratio of load to effort:

$$\text{MA} = \frac{\text{Load}}{\text{Effort}} \text{(no units)}$$

### *Velocity ratio (VR)*

Ratio of distance moved by effort to distance moved by load in equal times.

$$\text{VR} = \frac{\text{Distance effort moves}}{\text{Distance load moves}} \text{(no units)}$$

### *Efficiency*

Efficiency of a machine is:

$$\frac{\text{Energy output (at load)}}{\text{Energy input (at effort)}} \times 100\%$$

It is always less than 100%. It is reduced by friction.
Efficiency also equals $\text{MA/VR} \times 100\%$.

### *Friction*

Friction is the force which opposes the relative sliding motion between two surfaces. Fig. 2.15 shows forces acting on a block resting on a table when a small force ($T$) is applied. As the force increases the force of friction ($F$) also increases to oppose it – $F$ and $T$ act in opposite directions.

1 Maximum frictional force between two surfaces prior to

motion is called **limiting friction**. When $T$ exceeds this value the block moves.

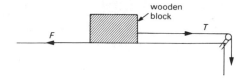

Fig. 2.15 *Friction*

2  The force $T$ needed to maintain motion once friction has been overcome is less than limiting friction, i.e. **static** friction is greater than **dynamic** friction.
3  The force of friction between two surfaces is:
   * independent of area of contact;
   * dependent on material and type of surface.

In machines, friction losses pose problems since work has to be done to overcome them. This directly affects mechanical advantage and efficiency. Friction can be reduced by lubrication.

# 3  WAVES

## General features of waves

1  Waves are produced by **vibrations** (periodic disturbances).
2  A wave is a **travelling** periodic disturbance – it transfers energy from one place to another.
3  Some waves need a medium to travel in, e.g. sound waves, waves on a spring, water waves.
4  **Electromagnetic** waves, e.g. light waves, radio waves, do *not* require a medium – they can travel through a vacuum.

### Transverse and longitudinal waves

1  A **transverse** wave – periodic disturbances are at right angles to direction of wave travel, e.g. light waves, water waves.
2  A **longitudinal** wave – periodic disturbances are in same direction as wave travel, e.g. sound waves.

### Describing a wave

A wave causes displacement as it travels. The features of a wave can be shown on a displacement–distance graph (see Fig. 3.1). Points A and B on the graph are in **phase**, i.e. they have the same speed and direction of movement.

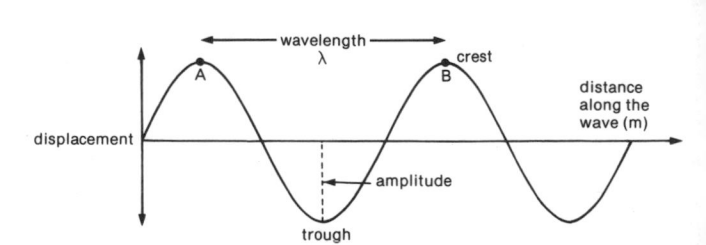

Fig. 3.1 *Displacement–distance graph for a wave*

1 The **frequency**(*f*) is the number of complete oscillations made every second (cycles per second) – measured in hertz (Hz).

2 The **wavelength** ($\lambda$, lambda) is the distance between two successive points at the same part of the cycle, i.e. the distance between identical parts of adjacent waves – measured in metres (m).

3 The **speed** (*v*) of a wave is the distance a wave front travels in unit time – measured in metres per second (m/s).

4 $v = f\lambda$

5 The **amplitude** is the maximum displacement from rest position caused by a wave.

### *Light waves and the electromagnetic spectrum*

Although light travels in straight lines through a continuous medium, its energy is transferred in the form of wave-like packets of energy (**photons**). Light waves have wavelengths ranging from $4 \times 10^{-7}$ to $7 \times 10^{-7}$ m (400–700 nm) and are part of the **electromagnetic spectrum** (see Fig. 3.2). Waves in the electromagnetic spectrum:

1 are transverse waves;

2 are progressive waves;

3 can travel in a vacuum;

4 have a speed of about $3 \times 10^8$ m/s in a vacuum.

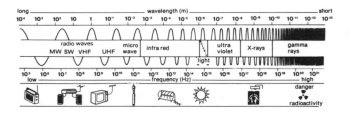

Fig. 3.2 *The electromagnetic spectrum*

29

As their wavelength becomes shorter the frequency gets higher (from the wave equation $v = f\lambda$). The higher the frequency (shorter wavelength) the more energetic the radiation.

1 Ultra-violet radiation is responsible for sun tan. It may be detected by photographic plates.
2 Infra-red radiation may be detected by a rise in temperature or by a thermopile.
3 Radio and television waves and radar can be detected by special receiving aerials.

## Water waves and the ripple tank

A ripple tank is a shallow tray of water. The water in a ripple tank may be set in motion by various vibrators or dippers. By viewing the resulting wave patterns produced by the disturbances and by placing various obstacles and reflecting surfaces in the tank it is possible to demonstrate **reflection**, **refraction**, **diffraction** and **interference** – the **properties of waves**.

### Reflection
1 **Plane waves at a plane surface** (see Fig. 3.3).

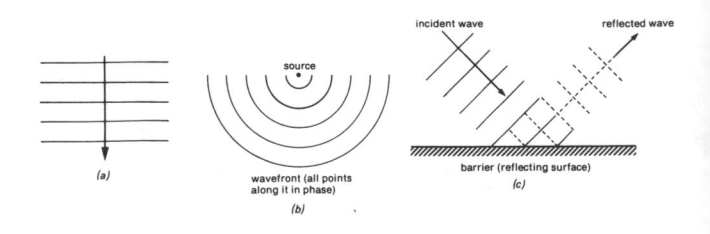

Fig. 3.3 (a) *Plane waves.* (b) *Circular waves.* (c) *Plane waves reflected by a barrier*

* Arrows show the direction of travel of progressing plane wavefront.
* Plane waves hit the plane reflecting barrier.
* Continuous lines show incident wavefronts, dotted lines show reflected waves.
* The laws of reflection hold.

## 2 Plane waves at curved surfaces (see Fig. 3.4).

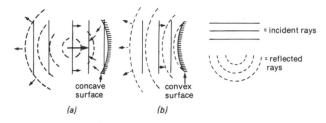

Fig. 3.4 *Plane waves at (a) concave surface (b) convex surface*

* A plane wave is brought to a focus by a concave surface (**converges**).
* A plane wave **diverges** (spreads out) at a convex surface.

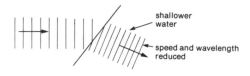

Fig. 3.5 *Refraction*

### Refraction
When plane water waves pass from deep to shallow water their wavelength becomes shorter. The frequency remains the same,

so from $v=f\lambda$ the speed must become less, i.e. the wavefront slows down. When the wavefront strikes a deep/shallow water boundary other than normally, the wavelength changes and the slowing down of the wavefront at the boundary causes a change in the direction the water travels (**refraction** – see Fig. 3.5).

### Diffraction

1 Waves passing through small gaps bend and spread out – **diffraction**.
2 If the gap is large compared to wavelength then the wavefront is only diffracted at its edges.
3 If the gap is small or about the same size as the wavelength, then the wavefront is circular and the waves spread out in all directions (see Fig. 3.6).

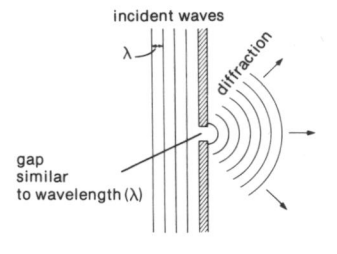

Fig. 3.6 *Diffraction at a slit*

The longer the wavelength the greater the diffraction, e.g. radio and sound waves easily bend around corners of buildings.

A **diffraction grating** consists of many diffracting gaps or slits. The gap size is chosen to be comparable with the wavelength of the incident waveform.

### Interference

If two point source dippers are connected to the same ripple-tank vibrator, the two sets of circular ripples will constructively and destructively interfere with each other (see Fig. 3.7).

1  **Constructive interference** occurs when two wavefronts meet at the same point at the same time, i.e. the two waves meet crest to crest and are therefore in phase. The vibration has twice the amplitude of a single wave at these points.
2  **Destructive interference** occurs when a crest meets a trough at the same point. The resulting amplitude of the wave is zero.

Fig. 3.7 *(a) Constructive and (b) destructive interference*

An interference pattern produced by two coherent point sources is shown in Fig. 3.8.

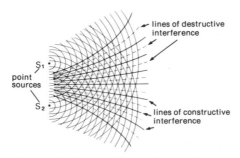

Fig. 3.8 *Interference with two coherent point sources*

1  Thick lines show where constructive interference occurs.
2  Dotted lines show where destructive interference occurs.
3  $S_1$ and $S_2$ are point centres of the disturbance and are

**coherent** – they have the same frequency, the same amplitude, and are in phase with each other.

### Interference of light – Young's slits

If two coherent light sources are allowed to interfere, constructive and destructive interference patterns (similar to water wave patterns) are produced. The arrangement is called Young's slits (see Fig. 3.9).

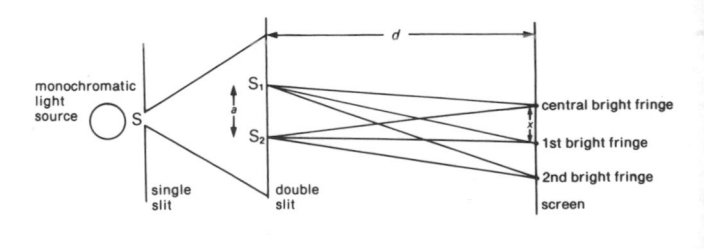

Fig. 3.9 *Young's slits*

1  The light source (S) is **monochromatic** (one frequency) from behind a single slit.
2  The coherent sources ($S_1$, $S_2$) are produced by allowing the wavefront from S to be incident on two slits. The slits are less than 1 mm apart.
3  The point sources ($S_1$, $S_2$) are at the same point on the wavefront; thus they are in phase and coherent.
4  The resulting interference pattern is observed on a screen. Bright bands of light (fringes) are seen.
5  The distance ($x$) between fringes is measured using a telescope eyepiece.
6  $\lambda = \dfrac{ax}{d}$

   where $\lambda$=wavelength of light used, $a$=distance between slits, $d$=distance from slits to screen.

Using Young's slits the wavelength of a light source, e.g. a laser, can be measured. The fringes come closer together as the wavelength of light increases, e.g. from red to blue.

# 4 LIGHT

## Rectilinear propagation

1  **Rectilinear propagation**=light transmitted in straight lines.
2  The path along which the light energy passes is a **ray**.
3  A collection of rays is a **beam**.
4  Light rays or beams are represented by straight lines, usually with an arrow to indicate direction.

### Shadows

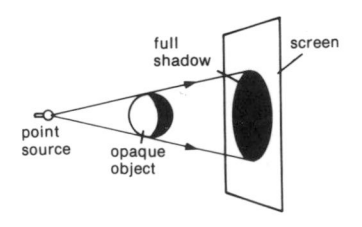

Fig. 4.1 *Shadow from a point source*

1  When an opaque obstacle is placed in the path of a point source of light, a clear **shadow** is produced (see Fig. 4.1).
2  A larger light source produces two regions of shadow (see Fig. 4.2): **umbra** (full shadow); and **penumbra** (part-shadow).

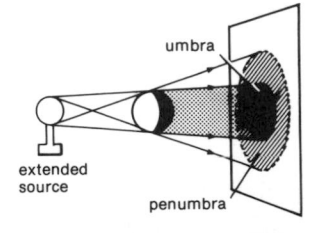

Fig. 4.2 *Shadow from an extended source*

### *Eclipses*

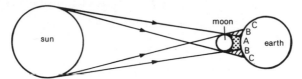

Fig. 4.3 *Eclipse of the sun*

1 An eclipse of the **sun** shows the sun as an extended source of light. The sun, moon and earth are in line, with the moon's shadow cast on the earth. An observer on earth sees:
   * a total eclipse (A in Fig. 4.3);
   * a partial eclipse (B);
   * no eclipse (C);
   depending on where he is situated.
2 In a **lunar** eclipse the earth's shadow falls on the moon and an observer on the moon would see no light from the sun – the observer would be in the total eclipse.

### *Pinhole camera*
This is a light-proof box with a pinhole at one end and a photographic film or translucent screen at the other. It shows the rectilinear propagation of light (see Fig. 4.4).

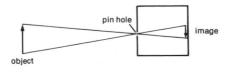

Fig. 4.4 *Pinhole camera*

### The speed of light

1  Light has a finite measurable speed, constant for any given optical medium.
2  Speed of light varies from medium to medium depending upon optical density.
3  Speed of light is greatest when passing through a vacuum (about $3.0 \times 10^8$ m/s).
4  Air has similar optical density to that of a vacuum and so influences the speed of light very little.
5  Water and glass have a greater optical density and so slow down light – speed of light in water and glass is about $2.3 \times 10^8$ and $2.0 \times 10^8$ m/s respectively.

## Reflection of light

1  Highly polished metal surfaces **reflect** nearly all incident light. A **mirror** is a good reflecting surface.
2  Matt surfaces **absorb** most incident light. The absorbed light energy **heats** the surface.
3  Regular reflection occurs when a parallel beam of light is incident on a flat or plane mirror and the reflected light remains parallel.
4  Diffuse reflection occurs when a parallel beam of light strikes an uneven reflecting surface.

### The laws of reflection

1  **Incident ray**, **normal** and the **reflected ray** all lie in the same plane and meet at a point (see Fig. 4.5).
2  The angle of incidence is equal to the angle of reflection:

$$i = r$$

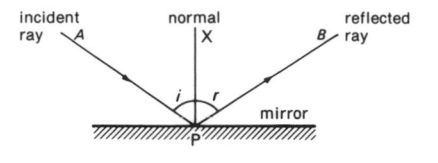

Fig. 4.5 *Laws of reflection*

The ray of light AP is the incident ray; it makes an angle of incidence ($i$) with the normal (PX). The ray of light PB is the reflected ray; the angle made between this ray and the normal is the angle of reflection ($r$). The normal is a line drawn at 90° to the mirror surface at the point where the incident ray strikes the surface. All angles are measured from this line to the rays.

1  A **real** image is one which can be formed on a screen.
2  A **virtual** image cannot be projected onto a screen. The image is formed at a point from which the rays appear to diverge after reflection.

### Images in plane mirrors

The image of an object seen in a flat or plane mirror is:
1  situated as far behind the mirror as the object is in front;
2  **virtual** – can't be projected onto a screen;
3  **laterally inverted** – appears opposite in nature to that of the object, e.g. right appears left.

Plane mirrors are used in periscopes, kaleidoscopes, sextants, measuring instruments (placing a flat mirror behind an instrument pointer reduces error in reading the scale).

### Curved mirrors

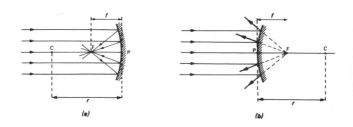

Fig. 4.6 *Reflection at (a) concave (b) convex mirror*

1   There are two basic types of curved mirror:
    *   **concave** mirrors **converge** parallel incident light after reflection;
    *   **convex** mirrors **diverge** parallel incident light after reflection.
2   Both may be considered as parts of spheres having a centre of curvature C and radius $r$.
3   The centre of the mirror is called the **pole** (P). A line from C to P which is normal to the mirror surface is the **principal axis**.
4   The **focal length** of a curved mirror ($f$) is equal to *half* the radius ($r$). i.e. $f = \frac{1}{2}r$.

### Images in concave mirrors

Images produced by concave mirrors can be found by graphical method (see Fig. 4.7). Two rays of light are drawn from the tip of an object.

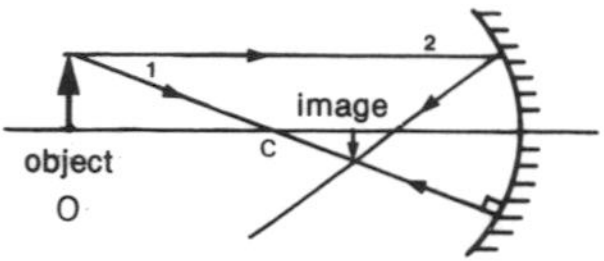

Fig. 4.7 *Ray diagram for a concave mirror*

1   A ray of light (1) passing through the centre of curvature (C), touching the tip of the object, strikes the mirror normally and is reflected back along the original ray.
2   A ray of light (2) travelling parallel to the principal axis, touching the tip of the object and striking the mirror, passes through the principal focus after reflection.

Using the graphical method it is possible to predict the nature, size and position of any image formed by a concave mirror for any object position (see Fig. 4.8).

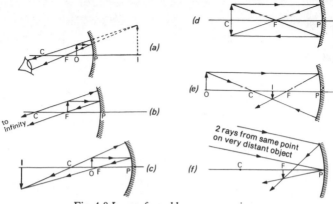

Fig. 4.8 *Images formed by a concave mirror*

1 Object **between F and P** (Fig. 4.8 (a)) – image is:
   ★ behind the mirror;
   ★ virtual;
   ★ erect;
   ★ larger than object.
2 Object **at F** (Fig. 4.8 (b)) – image is at infinity.
3 Object **between F and C** (Fig. 4.8 (c)) – image is:
   ★ beyond C;
   ★ real;
   ★ inverted;
   ★ larger than object.
4 Object **at C** (Fig. 4.8 (d)) – image is:
   ★ at C;
   ★ real;
   ★ inverted;
   ★ same size as object.
5 Object **beyond C** (Fig. 4.8 (e)) – image is:

- ★ between C and F;
- ★ real;
- ★ inverted;
- ★ smaller than object.
6 Object **at infinity** (Fig. 4.8 (f)) – image is:
  - ★ at F;
  - ★ real;
  - ★ inverted;
  - ★ smaller than object.

### Images in convex mirrors

A similar graphical method for finding the image can be used for convex mirrors.
1 The image produced for all object positions is virtual.
2 The focal point (F) and radius of curvature (C) are virtual.

| Position of object | Position of image | Nature of image |
|---|---|---|
| All except infinity | Virtual between F and P | Erect, |
| At infinity | Virtual at F | diminished |

### Magnification

The magnification produced by a mirror can be found from either:

1 Magnification $= \dfrac{\text{Image size}}{\text{Object size}}$

2 Magnification $= \dfrac{\text{Image distance from the mirror}}{\text{Object distance from the mirror}}$

### Parabolic mirrors

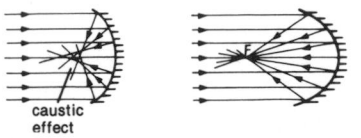

Fig. 4.9 (a) Concave mirror showing caustic effect. (b) Parabolic mirror

For most concave mirrors only rays of light close to, and parallel to, the principal axis pass through the principal focus after reflection. With wide aperture concave mirrors, the **caustic effect** is produced. A wide aperture with high optical accuracy demands **parabolic** mirrors (see Fig. 4.9).

## *Uses of curved mirrors*
1 Convex mirrors give wide angle of view, e.g. in supermarkets to detect shoplifters, on buses, as car wing mirrors.
2 Concave mirrors are **magnifiers**, e.g. shaving mirror, dentist's mirrors, make-up mirror.
3 Parabolic mirrors produce a parallel beam of light, e.g. car headlight, pocket torch.

## Refraction

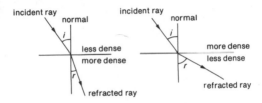

Fig. 4.10 *Refraction of a light ray*

Refraction is the bending of light as it crosses the boundary from one medium to another of different optical density.
1 Light passing from an optically less dense to an optically more dense medium is refracted **towards** the normal.
2 Light passing from an optically more dense to an optically less dense medium is refracted **away** from the normal.
3 Degree of bending of light depends on the relative optical densities of the two media.

## *The laws of refraction*
1 Incident ray, refracted ray and the normal at the point of incidence all lie in the same plane.

2  Ratio of the sine of the angle of incidence ($i$) to the sine of the angle of refraction ($r$) is constant for a given pair of media (**Snell's law**):

$$\frac{\text{Sin } i}{\text{Sin } r} = n \text{ (a constant)}$$

3  $n$ is the refractive index – it has no units, e.g. for water $n = 1.33$, for glass $n = 1.5$.

4  Another way of expressing $n$:

$$n \text{ for medium} = \frac{\text{Speed of light in air}}{\text{Speed of light in that medium}}$$

### *Refraction in a glass block*

Tracing a light ray through a rectangular glass block shows refraction at the air/glass and glass/air surfaces. The emerging ray travels parallel to the initial incident ray but is **displaced** to one side (see Fig. 4.11).

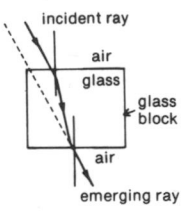

Fig. 4.11 *Refraction in a glass block*

### *Real and apparent depth*

Objects seen through liquid or glass often *appear* to be closer than they really are, i.e. their **apparent** depth is less than their **real** depth, e.g. when looking through a glass block, a swimming pool or water in a pond. It is caused by refraction:

$$\frac{\text{Real depth}}{\text{Apparent depth}} = n \text{ of material looked through}$$

### Total internal reflection and critical angle

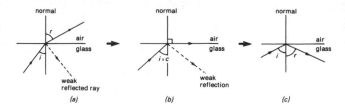

Fig. 4.12 (a) Angle of incidence less than critical angle. (b) $i = c$. Refracted ray is at 90° to normal. (c) Total internal reflection

1  Total internal reflection occurs when a ray of light travelling in an optical medium strikes the boundary of an optically less dense medium at an angle greater than the critical angle.
2  The **critical angle** is the angle at which the incident ray of light strikes the boundary causing a refracted ray in the optically less dense medium to make an angle of 90° with the normal.
3  In practice achieving a refracted ray at 90° is difficult.
4  The critical angle can also be defined as the angle of incidence which is just less than that needed to cause total internal reflection.

$$\sin c = \frac{1}{{}_a n_g}$$

or

$$_a n_g = \frac{1}{\sin c}$$

where $_a n_g$ indicates that light passes from air to glass.
6  For a refractive index of 1.5 the critical angle for:
   ★ glass is about 42°;
   ★ for water is about 48°.

### Using total internal reflection

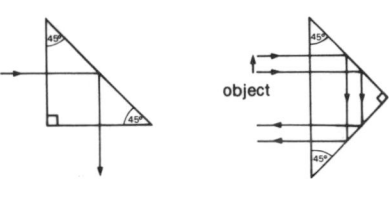

Fig. 4.13 *Total internal reflection in prisms – light turned through (a) 90°*
*(b) 180°*

Total internal reflection in right-angled prisms can turn light
through 90° or 180° (see Fig. 4.13). Prisms have advantages over
mirrors.

1 A greater proportion of incident light is reflected without
   scattering and absorption.
2 Glass mirrors have multiple reflections:
   ★ within the glass; and
   ★ between the glass and silvered backing;
   giving poor definition. Prisms do not have this problem.

Reflecting prisms are used in periscopes, binoculars and single-
lens reflex cameras.

### Dispersion, colour and the spectrum

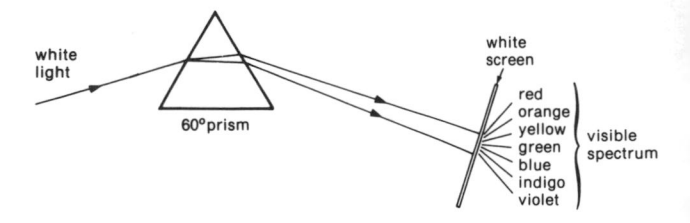

Fig. 4.14 *Dispersion of white light by a prism*

White light passed through a 60° prism is split into the colours of the visible spectrum (**dispersion** – see Fig. 4.14).

1 Dispersion occurs because each colour has its own refractive index. Red light is refracted the least – its refractive index is less than that of violet light, which is refracted the most.
2 A **pure** spectrum is produced by including a converging lens between the light source and the prism.
3 The seven colours recombine to form white light by passing the spectrum through an inverted 60° prism (see Fig. 4.15).

Fig. 4.15 *Recombining the spectrum*

### Lenses

1 A **convex** (converging) lens brings parallel incident light to a focus after refraction.
2 A **concave** (diverging) lens spreads out or diverges the incident parallel light. If traced back the diverging rays have a virtual focus.

### *Features of lenses*

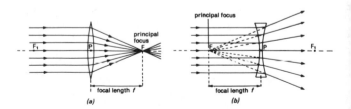

Fig. 4.16 *(a) Convex (converging) (b) concave (diverging) lenses*

1  The **principal axis** is a line passing through the **optical centre** (P). It strikes the lens normally.
2  Every lens has two principal foci, one on each side of the optical centre (F and $F_1$).
3  The distance between the optical centre and the principal focus is the **focal length** ($f$ – measured in cm or m).
4  Power of lens $= \dfrac{1}{f}$ dioptres

### *Images in converging lenses*
1  **Graphical method** – two rays of light are drawn from the tip of an object such that:
   *  a ray of light touching the tip of an object passes through the optical centre undeviated;
   *  a ray of light touching the tip of an object and travelling close to and parallel to the principal axis will pass through the principal focus after refraction.
   The position of the image is where the two refracted rays meet (see Fig. 4.17).

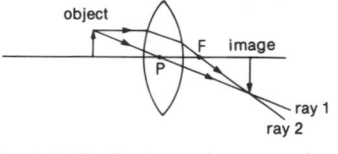

Fig. 4.17 *Finding images in a convex lens*

2  Using the **lens formula** and calculating the image position:
$$\frac{1}{u} + \frac{1}{v} = \frac{1}{f}$$
where $u=$ object distance (distance between optical centre and object), $v=$ image distance (distance between optical centre and image), $f=$ focal length of lens.

48

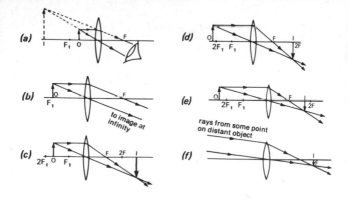

Fig. 4.18 *Images formed by a convex lens.*

- ★ If image produced is **real**, $v$ is **positive**.
- ★ If image produced is **virtual**, $v$ is **negative**.
- ★ If lens is **convex**, $f$ is **positive**.
- ★ If lens is **concave**, $f$ is **negative**.

Using the graphical method it is possible to predict the nature, size and position of any image formed for any object position (see Fig. 4.18).

1 Object **between lens and F** (Fig. 4.18(a)) – image is:
   - ★ behind the object;
   - ★ virtual
   - ★ erect;
   - ★ larger than object.
2 Object **at F** (Fig. 4.18(b)) – image is at infinity.
3 Object **between F and 2F** (Fig. 4.18(c)) – image is:
   - ★ beyond 2F;
   - ★ real;
   - ★ inverted;

49

★ larger than object.
4 Object **at 2F** (Fig. 4.18(d)) – image is:
  ★ at 2F;
  ★ real;
  ★ inverted;
  ★ same size as object.
5 Object **beyond 2F** (Fig. 4.18(e)) – image is:
  ★ between F and 2F;
  ★ real;
  ★ inverted;
  ★ smaller than object.
6 Object **at infinity** (Fig. 4.18(f)) – image is:
  ★ at F;
  ★ real;
  ★ inverted;
  ★ smaller than object.

The **magnification** produced by a lens is calculated from:

1 Magnification $= \dfrac{\text{Image size}}{\text{Object size}}$

2 Magnification $= \dfrac{v}{u}$

### Measuring f for a convex lens

1 Focus a distant object on a screen – as the object distance is close to infinity, $1/v = 1/f$, so $v$ is numerically equal to the focal length (a quick but not very accurate method).

2 Using an illuminated object, lens and plane mirror, produce a real inverted image beside the object (see Fig. 4.19). Again $v = f$.

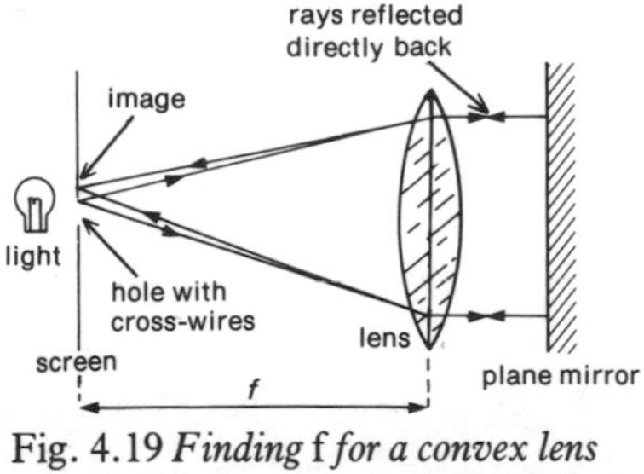

Fig. 4.19 *Finding f for a convex lens*

50

### *Images formed by concave lenses*

A similar graphical method for finding the image applies for both converging and diverging lenses, but for a diverging lens:

1 a ray of light parallel to the principal axis appears to pass through the virtual focal point;

2 the image formed is always:
   * virtual;
   * smaller than the object;
   * upright (erect);

for all object positions.

## Optical instruments

### *The human eye*

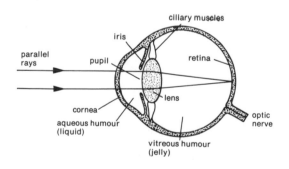

Fig. 4.20 *Human eye*

1 Light enters eye via **cornea** and passes through **lens**.

2  It is focused on the light-sensitive **retina**.
3  Nerve endings at the retina transmit messages via optic nerve to brain where they are interpreted.
4  **Aqueous humour** – transparent liquid between lens and cornea.
5  **Vitreous humour** – transparent jelly-like substance within the main body of the eye.
6  **Iris** – the coloured part of the eye which adjusts the pupil size; regulates amount of light entering the eye by reducing or increasing the size of the pupil.

The ability of the lens to focus light from near or far objects is **accommodation**. The **ciliary muscles** make the lens fatter to see near objects and thinner to see distant objects

## The magnifying glass

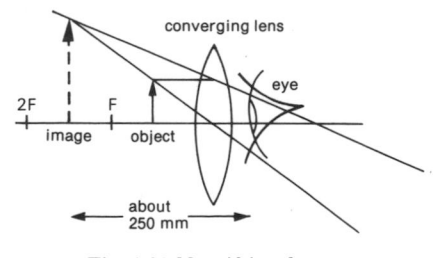

Fig. 4.21 *Magnifying glass*

1  A short focal-length converging lens is used.
2  The object to be magnified is placed between the optical centre and the principal focus of the lens.
3  Object adjusted to give visual, erect, magnified image at near point of distinct vision (about 250mm from eye – see Fig. 4.21).

### The lens camera

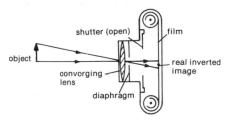

Fig. 4.22 *Simple lens camera*

1  A simple lens camera produces a small inverted, real image on light sensitive film at the back of the camera.
2  Correct exposure of the film depends on:
   ⋆ **shutter speed** – shutter briefly allows incident light to enter camera;
   ⋆ **diaphragm setting** controls aperture (opening);
   ⋆ type of **film** – ASA or DIN value gives speed of film.
3  To focus objects at varying distances from camera the lens has to be moved with respect to the film – controlled by the focussing ring.
   ⋆ For distant objects the distance between lens and film is equal to $f$ of lens.
   ⋆ As object is moved closer to camera the lens has to be moved away from film to maintain focus.
   ⋆ Correct lens position for each object distance is usually engraved on lens mounting.

| Eye | Camera | Comments |
|-----|--------|----------|
| Lens | Lens | Lens moved manually on camera to focus objects at varying distances. Eye lens alters automatically. |
| Iris | Diaphragm | Eye iris adjusts automatically. Camera iris is usually adjusted manually. |

| Eye | Camera | Comments |
|---|---|---|
| — | Shutter | Eye does not require a shutter since retina can be continually exposed to light. |
| Retina | Film | Film can only be exposed to light once, but keeps a permanent record. |

## Telescopes
1 **Astronomical** telescope uses two converging lenses, one of short and one of long focal length.
2 Newtonian **reflecting** telescope uses a large concave mirror, small plane mirror and a converging lens.
3 Both types of telescope give inverted image.
4 **Radio** telescopes focus incoming radio waves onto a receiving aerial using a parabolic reflector.

# 5   SOUND

## Sound waves

### Features of sound waves
1   Sound waves are produced by **vibrations**.
2   Sound waves are **longitudinal**.
    * Longitudinal waves are transmitted at a finite speed.
    * They travel in all directions from the vibrating source.
    * Direction of vibration same as direction of wave travel.
3   The energy of a sound wave is transferred by a series of compressions and rarefactions.
    * **Compressions** are high-density regions of the wave.
    * **Rarefactions** are low-density regions of the wave.
4   Each particle vibrates with the same amplitude and frequency about its mean position.
5   Sound waves can be detected by:
    * ear – translates vibrations into nerve impulses;
    * microphone – translates vibration into electrical impulses.
6   Sounds need an **elastic** medium through which to travel – *cannot* travel in a vacuum.
7   Sound waves can travel in solids, liquids and gases.
    * Speed of sound in liquids and solids is greater than in gases, e.g. air.
    * Sound waves in liquids, e.g. echo-sounding equipment – water depth determined by measuring time taken for sound transmitted from ship to be reflected off seabed and received back at ship.
    * Sound waves in solids, e.g. tapping metal rail and hearing sound at other end.

### Properties of sound waves
1   For a given frequency ($f$) and wavelength ($\lambda$), the speed of sound in a given medium is:
    $$v = f\lambda$$
2   Sound waves are **reflected** at hard non-porous surfaces, producing echoes.
    * Reflection at concave surfaces focuses sound waves.

* ★ Reflection at convex surfaces spreads out the sound.
* ★ In all conditions the laws of reflection hold.
* ★ The reflecting/absorbing qualities of materials affect the acoustics of rooms and concert halls.

3 Sound waves can be **refracted**, since they travel at different speeds according to acoustical density of medium.
* ★ Laws of refraction hold.
* ★ Critical angle and total internal reflection apply.

4 Sound waves can be **diffracted**, e.g. by domestic objects.

5 When two or more sound waves of same frequency overlap, interference occurs (see Fig. 5.1).
* ★ Two loudspeakers connected to same audio frequency generator (coherent sources).
* ★ Ear is moved parallel to but at a distance from the loud-speakers.
* ★ Interference patterns heard as loud (x) and soft (y) sounds – constructive and destructive interference.

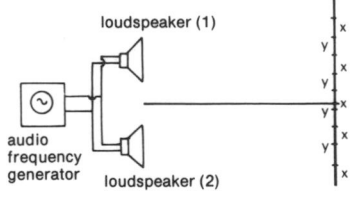

Fig. 5.1 *Interference of sound*

### The speed of sound in air

1 The speed of sound in air increases with temperature but is not affected by pressure. At 0 °C, in:
* ★ dry air the speed of sound is 330 m/s;
* ★ water 1,400 m/s.

2 It can be measured by finding the time taken for a sound to travel a measured distance:

$$\text{Speed of sound} = \frac{\text{Distance travelled}}{\text{Time taken}} \quad \text{in m/s}$$

## Sound and music

Sounds can be divided roughly into two types:
1 musical sounds or regular vibrations; and
2 non-musical sounds or random vibrations.

Musical notes vary in:
1 **pitch**;
2 **loudness**;
3 **quality**.

### Pitch

1 Pitch (like colour in light) is characterized by frequency.
   ★ High frequency gives a high-pitched note.
   ★ Low frequency gives a low-pitched note.
2 Human audio frequency hearing range is about 10–20 kHz (can be much reduced with age).
3 Ultrasound above 20 kHz – used in hospitals, depth sounding, by bats as form of radar, and heard by dogs.
4 If two notes are an **octave** apart in pitch, one note is **double** the frequency of the other.

### Loudness and intensity

1 The loudness of a sound depends on the **amplitude** of the sound wave.
2 Loudness is subjective; it is related to **intensity**.
   ★ Intensity of a sound wave is the range of flow of energy per unit area of the medium through which it passes.
   ★ The greater the intensity the louder the sound, e.g. very loud sounds have an intensity of about $1 \, W/m^2$.

### Quality

1 An oscilloscope displays incoming sound waves on a fluorescent screen. The wave pattern on the screen is called a **waveform**.
2 A piano and violin produce notes of *same* frequency and intensity, but the notes produce *different* sounds.
   ★ They have a different **quality**.
   ★ Both notes have the same **fundamental** frequency, but other weaker frequencies (**overtones**) are also present.

- ★ Overtones influence waveform produced by different instruments (see Fig. 5.2).

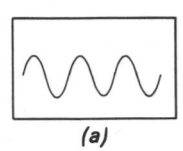 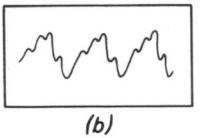 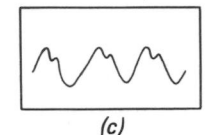

| (a) | (b) | (c) |

Fig. 5.2 *Waveforms produced by
(a) tuning fork (b) piano (c) guitar*

## *Beats*

If two notes of almost equal frequency are sounded together, the loudness of the resulting sound can be heard to rise and fall. The variations in sound are **beats** – caused by interference of the two sound waves. The waves go alternately *in* and *out* of phase with each other, leading to alternate **constructive** then **destructive** interference. The closer the two frequencies, the longer the time between beats.

## Vibrations in strings and air columns

### *Stationary waves*

1 If a long string, fixed at one end, is quickly vibrated at the other, a wave pattern progresses along it from the source of disturbance – a **progressive** wave.

2 A **stationary** wave is formed when a progressive wave is reflected back from the fixed position. Two equal progressive waves are then superimposed on one another when travelling in opposite directions.

3 Along a stationary wave points of:
  - ★ maximum oscillation are **antinodes**;
  - ★ points of zero oscillation are **nodes**.

### Strings

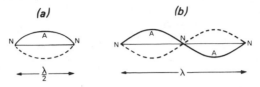

Fig. 5.3 *Stationary waves on a string. (a) Fundamental frequency.*
*(b) First overtone*

A string, fixed at one end and vibrated at the other at a constant frequency, vibrates in a series of equal 'segments', due to antinodes (A) and nodes (N). The number of 'segments' depends upon frequency of vibration. In the simplest mode of vibration a string vibrates in a single segment – the **fundamental** ($f_o$). The length of this fundamental is equal to **half** the wavelength of the progressing wave. Factors that affect the fundamental frequency of a vibrating string are:

1  **tension** ($T$) – the tighter the string the higher the frequency;
2  **length** ($l$) – doubling the length halves the frequency;
3  **mass per unit length** ($m$) – a thick heavy string vibrates more slowly than a light thin one.
4  The formula for the fundamental frequency of a string is:

$$f = \frac{1}{2l} \sqrt{\frac{T}{m}}$$

### Air columns
Standing or stationary waves also occur in columns of air in pipes (see Fig. 5.4).

1  Vibrations in a column of air are longitudinal (*not* transverse as in a string).
2  Doubling the length of an air column halves the frequency.

### Resonance
1  **Resonance** occurs when a body or system is set into oscillation at its own natural frequency as a result of some other vibrating system oscillating with the same frequency.

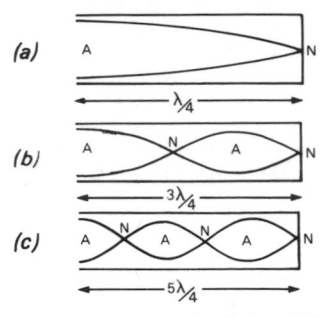

Fig. 5.4 *Stationary waves in closed pipe.* (a) *Fundamental.*
(b) *First overtone.* (c) *Second overtone*

2  If a tuning fork is sounded near the open end of a pipe,
   **resonance** occurs if the frequency of the fork is the same as
   the natural frequency of vibration of the air column (see Fig.
   5.5).

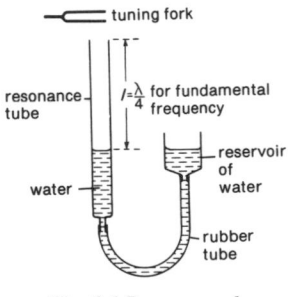

Fig. 5.5 *Resonance tube*

3  This apparatus can be used to measure the speed of sound
   using the equation $v = f\lambda$.
4  Resonance can occur with all kinds of periodic disturbances
   or waves, e.g. radio waves, vibrations in a car, bus or
   aeroplane, the wind.

Moving molecules of all solids, liquids and gases possess both kinetic *and* potential energy – their **thermal energy**. Heating occurs when thermal energy is transferred from one body to another.

### Temperature and thermometers
1  Thermal energy of an object increases with **temperature**.
2  Thermal energy is transferred from a body at higher temperature to a body at lower temperature until their temperatures become equal.
3  Thermal energy transferred is often called **heat**.

### *Temperature scales*
1  Temperature is the degree of hotness of a body, measured by a **thermometer**.
2  Two **fixed points** are needed to form a temperature scale:
   ★  **ice point**;
   ★  **steam point**.
3  Thermometer to be graduated is first placed in pure melting ice – when the liquid in the thermometer has reached a steady position, the **lower fixed point** (ice point of water) is observed and marked on the scale.

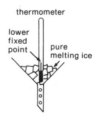

Fig. 6.1 *Lower fixed point*

**4 Upper fixed point** is the boiling point of pure water at standard atmospheric pressure (760 mm of mercury).

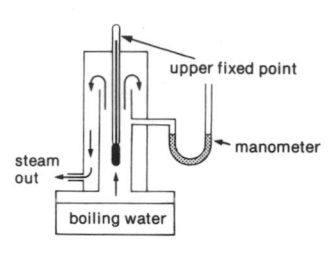

Fig. 6.2 *Upper fixed point*

### Celsius and Kelvin scales

1 On the Celsius scale the:
  * lower fixed point is 0 °C;
  * upper fixed point is 100 °C.
2 The Celsius scale is divided into **100** equal divisions between the upper and lower fixed points.
3 The lowest temperature an object can reach is **absolute zero** – this is zero on the absolute (Kelvin) scale.
4 The temperature interval is the same for both Celsius and Kelvin scales.
  * $-273\,°C = 0\,K$
  * $0\,°C = 273\,K$
  * $100\,°C = 373\,K$
5 The kelvin is an SI unit – it is *wrong* to write °K.

### Liquid-in-glass thermometers

1 All thermometers use a physical property of a certain material which changes with temperature.
2 The most common thermometers are liquid-in-glass thermometers.
  * They consist of a liquid enclosed in a glass tube.
  * The liquid (usually **mercury** or **alcohol**) expands or con-

tracts with temperature change, moving up and down the central capillary tube.

★ The higher the temperature the greater the expansion of the liquid up the capillary tube.

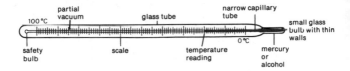

Fig. 6.3 *Liquid-in-glass thermometer*

|  | Mercury | Alcohol |
|---|---|---|
| Advantages | Conducts heat well | Suitable for low temperatures – freezes at −115 °C |
|  | Does not 'wet' the glass |  |
|  | Visible, reflects light |  |
|  | Does not boil until about 350 °C | Greater expansion than mercury |
| Disadvantages | Expensive | Low boiling point, 78 °C |
|  | Freezes at −39 °C | Needs colouring to be visible |
|  | Poisonous | 'Wets' the sides of the tube |

3  Water is *unsuitable* as a thermometric liquid because:
   ★ it contracts when warmed from 0 °C to 4 °C;
   ★ it has a small temperature range, i.e. 0 °C to 100 °C only.

4  The **clinical thermometer** is used to measure human body temperatures.
   ★ Its range is from 35–43 °C.
   ★ Its capillary tube has a constriction to stop the mercury returning to the bulb until it is shaken (see Fig. 6.4).

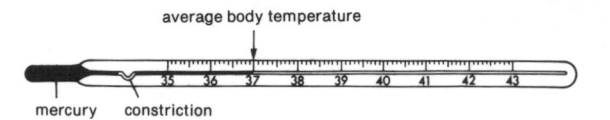

average body temperature

mercury    constriction

Fig. 6.4 *Clinical thermometer*

5  Liquid-in-glass thermometers are often unsuitable for industry. **Thermocouple** thermometers are used to measure oven and furnace temperatures. Their range is from about $-200°C–1,600°C$.

## Expansion of solids and liquids

With a few exceptions all substances **expand** when heated and **contract** when cooled. Heating a substance gives its molecules more energy; this extra energy leads to expansion.

### Expansion of solids

1  The expansion of any solid is *small* per degree rise in temperature compared to its original size. However the expansion and contraction of solids can set up enormous forces.

2  The **linear expansivity** of a solid is the fraction of its original length by which a length of that solid increases for a $1 K$ ($1°C$) rise in temperature:

$$\text{Linear expansivity} = \frac{\text{Increase in length}}{\text{Original length} \times \text{Temperature rise}}$$

It is a *very* small number, e.g. for steel, linear expansivity = $0.000011/°C$ (or K).

3  Different solids expand by different amounts when heated by same amount, i.e. they have different linear expansivities.

4  Linear expansivity of a metal rod can be measured by heating it with steam and measuring its increase in length (see Fig. 6.5).

5  Using expansion of solids.
   ★ Steel tyres can be fitted by heating them and then allowing them to contract tightly onto a wheel.
   ★ Two strips of metal with different expansivities, e.g. brass and steel, can be joined together to form a bimetallic strip.

64

This bends when heated. This bending can be used to switch on and off an electric circuit (see Fig. 6.6).

★ Bimetal strips used in fire alarms, flashing car indicators, bimetal thermometers.

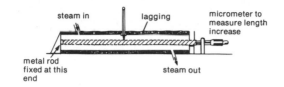

Fig. 6.5 *Measuring linear expansivity*

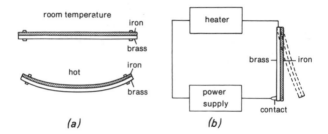

Fig. 6.6 (a) *Bimetal strip* (b) *acting as a thermostat in an electric circuit*

### Expansion of liquids

When liquids expand their volume increases and their density decreases. Different liquids expand by different amounts when heated.

1 Several identical flasks fitted with identical thin glass tubes are filled with different liquids and placed in same water bath.
2 Liquid levels adjusted so that for an initial temperature they are all the same.
3 Water bath is heated and stirred to ensure that each flask is at same temperature.

**4** At a new, higher temperature some liquids will have expanded more than others.

### Unusual expansion of water

When water is heated from 0°C to 4°C it **contracts** and its density increases. Its maximum density occurs at 4°C. In winter the water in a pond at 4°C sinks to the bottom – this is why ponds rarely freeze up completely.

### The gas laws

Gases expand much more than liquids or solids. The different relations between:

**1 pressure;**
**2 temperature;**
**3 volume;**

are called the **gas laws**.

### Variation of volume with pressure at constant temperature

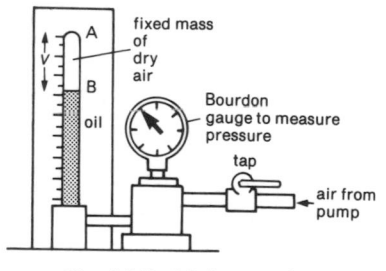

Fig. 6.7 *Boyle's law experiment*

**1** Air is trapped above a column of oil.
**2** Its volume ($V$) is proportional to AB (see Fig. 6.7)
**3** Pressure is applied by a pump and transmitted through the oil to the air.
**4** Pressure ($P$) is read directly from a Bourdon gauge.
**5** Various values of $P$ and $V$ are measured (temperature *must* remain constant).

6  A graph of pressure ($P$) against volume ($V$) is plotted.
7  Another graph of $P$ against $1/V$ is also plotted – **roughly a straight line.**

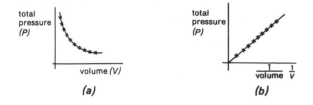

*(a)*    *(b)*

Fig. 6.8 *Graphs obtained in Boyle's law experiment*

8  From the graphs (see Fig. 6.8), for any given pairs of $P$ and $V$;
   $$P V = k$$
   where $k$ is a constant.
9  **Boyle's law** – volume of a fixed mass of gas is inversely proportional to the pressure, if the temperature remains constant.

### *Variation of volume with temperature at constant pressure*

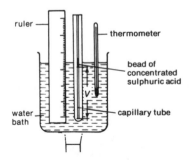

Fig. 6.9 *Charles' law experiment*

1 A fixed mass of air in a glass tube is heated in a water bath.
2 After heating, values of temperature $(T)$ and volume $(V)$ are noted at intervals.
3 Before readings are taken the air is allowed sufficient time to expand to a value appropriate to the new temperature.
4 As with Boyle's law, $V$ is not the true volume but if a tube of uniform cross-sectional area is used then the volume is proportional to the length of air measured (external pressure *must* remain constant).
5 Graphs of $V$ against $T$ are plotted – $V$ is directly proportional to absolute temperature (see Fig. 6.10).

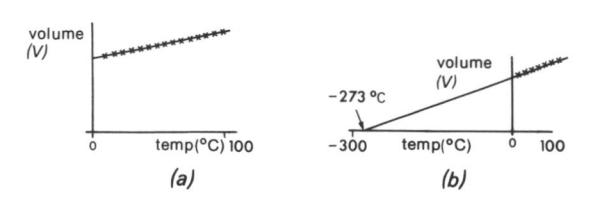

Fig. 6.10 *Graphs from Charles' law experiment.* (*a*) $V \propto T$.
(*b*) *Graph extended backwards*

6 **Charles law** – volume of a fixed mass of gas at constant pressure expands by 1/273 of its original volume at 0 °C per degree rise in temperature.
7 For any given pairs of $V$ and $T$ the volume of gas at constant pressure is proportional to its absolute temperature:

$$\frac{V}{T} = k$$

where $k$ is constant and $T$ is temperature in kelvin.

### Variation of pressure with temperature at constant volume

1 A gas is heated in a closed flask. It expands and the manometer liquid is forced round the tube from A.
2 Manometer levels are adjusted to bring liquid back to A to maintain constant volume.

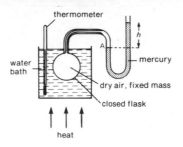

Fig. 6.11 *Pressure law experiment*

3 Pressure exerted by gas is then equal to atmospheric pressure
$H$ (mmHg) + $h$ (mmHg – difference in manometer levels).

4 As temperature is increased the manometer liquid levels must
be readjusted to A to maintain constant volume.

5 Values of $P$ ($=H+h$) against $T$ are plotted (see Fig. 6.12).

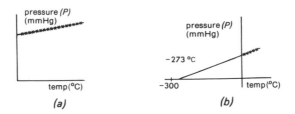

Fig. 6.12 *Graphs from pressure law experiment*
(*a*) $P \propto T$. (*b*) *Graph extended backwards*

6 **Pressure law** – pressure exerted by a fixed mass of gas at
constant volume increases by 1/273 of its original volume at
0 °C per degree rise in temperature.

7 For any given pairs of $P$ and $T$ the pressure exerted by a gas at
constant volume is proportional to its absolute temperature:

$$\frac{P}{T} = k$$

where $k$ is constant and $T$ is temperature in kelvin.

8 Graphs produced by pressure law show remarkable similarity to those produced by Charles' law.

9 Pressure law can be explained by kinetic theory.
  ★ As gas temperature rises, molecules move faster.
  ★ They bombard container with greater and greater force.
  ★ If gas is not allowed to expand, its pressure increases (because of molecular bombardment).

## The general gas equation

The three gas laws:

| Boyle's law | $PV = k$ |
|---|---|
| Charles' law | $V/T = k$ |
| pressure law | $P/T = k$ |

can be combined to produce the general equation:

$$\frac{PV}{T} = k \text{ (a constant)}$$

This can be stated as:

$$\frac{P_1 V_1}{T_1} = \frac{P_2 V_2}{T_2}$$

where $P_1$, $V_1$ and $T_1$ are the pressure, volume and *absolute* temperature of a gas before any change and $P_2$, $V_2$ and $T_2$ are its pressure, volume and *absolute* temperature after a change.

## Heat transfer

Thermal energy can be transferred from a hotter body to a colder one by:

1 **conduction**;
2 **convection**;
3 **radiation**.

## Conduction

How well a material transfers heat determines whether it is a good **conductor** or **insulator**. A material conducts heat at a rate depending upon its **thermal conductivity**. Thermal conductivities can be compared by heating the ends of several waxed rods of similar size but different materials in a water bath. As the water temperature increases, the thermal conductivity of the rods can be compared by measuring the length of melted wax on each rod after a few minutes (see Fig. 6.13).

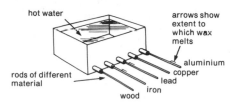

Fig. 6.13 *Comparing conductivity*

1 Metals conduct heat better than non-metals.
2 Some metals are better conductors than others – copper is about eight times better than steel.
3 Liquids (except mercury) and gases are generally bad conductors – place a weighted piece of ice at the bottom of a test tube of water; the water is heated vigorously at its surface; even though water boils at top of tube, ice does not melt any faster than it would at room temperature.
4 Conductors are used for saucepans, kettles, wire gauze and hot plates.
5 Insulators are used to reduce heat loss, e.g. wool, fibreglass, air.

### How conduction occurs

Good conductors of heat are also good conductors of electricity. They contain **free electrons** which help to transfer thermal energy more quickly. Poor conductors, e.g. non-metals, conduct heat by the vibrations of their atoms only.

### Convection

Heat is 'carried' through a fluid (liquids or gases) by convection currents.

71

1 Convection currents in water can be demonstrated by heating a small crystal of potassium permanganate placed near the side of a beaker of still water. Dye traces are produced which show the direction of convection currents.
   * Small masses of water receive energy, expand and become less dense.
   * Being less dense they rise and cooler water takes their place.
   * After a while these masses cool down, become more dense and sink.
2 Convection in water is used in domestic hot water systems.
3 Convection currents in air are involved in:
   * land and sea breezes – in daytime land warms up quickly due to heat from the sun, causing air above land to rise and set up convection currents bringing cool breezes from sea; at night the reverse occurs as the sea retains more heat than land; convection currents are now set up over the sea creating a warm breeze onto the land (see Fig. 6.14); convection currents influence weather and climate.

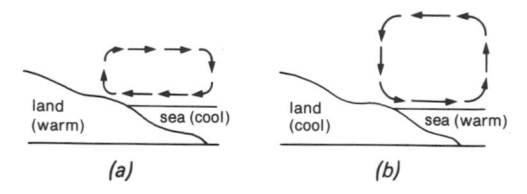

Fig. 6.14 *Land and sea breezes. (a) Day. (b) Night*

   * warming a room – most room heaters (including 'radiators') warm air by convection currents; warm air above heater rises, cooler air takes its place; circulating air carries heat around the room.

### Radiation
1 Radiation is transmission of energy by electromagnetic wave motion. Much hot-body radiation is in infra-red region of

electromagnetic spectrum.

2 Infra-red and light waves have similar properties:
   * travel in straight lines;
   * travel at the same speed – $3 \times 10^8$ m/s in a vacuum;
   * can be reflected and refracted;
   * can be absorbed by black/dull surface and reflected by shiny ones.

3 Infra-red radiation can be detected by:
   * photographic plate (by affecting the emulsion);
   * thermometer with blackened bulb to absorb the radiation;
   * thermopile – produces electric current; consists of many thermocouples connected in series; a thermocouple consists of two metals which, when placed in contact, produce an electric current which increases with temperature, e.g. copper with iron, antimony with bismuth.

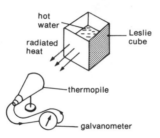

Fig. 6.15 *Thermal radiation from different surfaces*

4 A thermopile, when connected to a galvanometer and pointed towards a Leslie cube, can be used to compare radiation emitted from the different surface materials of the cube. This experiment shows that:
   * black/dull surfaces are good radiating surfaces when hot, and good absorbing surfaces when cold;
   * shiny, polished surfaces are bad radiating surfaces when hot, and bad absorbing surfaces when cold.

5 Remember that:

* good radiating surfaces are good absorbers and bad reflectors;
* bad radiating surfaces are bad absorbers and good reflectors.

### Some applications of radiation and its properties

1 Banks of solar cells are used to power electrical apparatus, e.g. space satellites, watches, calculators.
2 Dark painted, matt finished cars and dark coloured clothing absorb heat.
3 Light coloured, shiny surfaces reflect heat – sportsmen wear white clothing to keep cool.
4 Roofs of buildings may be painted with shiny reflecting paints; during the day the sun's energy is reflected whilst at night interior heat is allowed to escape; interior is therefore kept at a steady temperature.
5 Solar heating panels – black/matt surfaces absorb energy from sun's rays and transfer it to water pipes.
6 **Greenhouse effect** – glass is transparent to short, higher energy, infra-red radiation and opaque to longer radiation emitted by cooler bodies, so a greenhouse acts as a **heat trap**; shorter-wave radiation from the sun can get in but reflected rays at lower energy and longer wavelength cannot get out; there is therefore a rise in temperature in the greenhouse.

### The vacuum flask

A hot body can remain hot, and a cold body cold, for a long time if heat transfer by conduction, convection and radiation can be

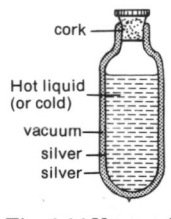

cork

Hot liquid (or cold)

vacuum

silver
silver

Fig. 6.16 *Vacuum flask*

reduced. This is achieved in a vacuum (Thermos) flask (see Fig. 6.16).

1 **Conduction** – reduced as very little heat can pass across the glass-formed vacuum flask. The stopper (usually double sealed) is also of a material of low thermal conductivity.
2 **Convection** – eliminated since the space between the two glass-formed flask walls is almost a vacuum.
3 Flask walls are silvered to reduce heat **radiation** – inner surface reflects back heat to contents and outer wall reflects back all external incident radiation.

## Specific heat capacity

### Heat capacity and specific heat
1 Heat is measured in joules (J).
2 The heat capacity of an object is the number of joules needed to raise its temperature by 1 K (1 °C). It is measured in J/K.
3 The specific heat capacity of a substance ($c$) is the number of joules needed to raise the temperature of 1 kg of the substance by 1 K (1 °C). It is measured in J/(kg K), e.g. copper's specific heat capacity, $c = 400$ J/(kg K), water $c = 4,200$ J/(kg K).

### Heat calculations
Heat needed to produce a temperature rise depends on:
1 **mass** of the substance;
2 its **specific heat capacity**;
3 the **rise in temperature**.
4 Heat required = Mass × Specific heat capacity × Temperature change.

$$= m \times c \times (\theta_2 - \theta_1)$$

where $\theta_1$ and $\theta_2$ are the temperatures before and after.
5 If a substance loses heat the same formula applies.

### Measuring specific heat capacity

1 For a **solid** (see Fig. 6.17).
   ★ Electric immersion heater placed in solid block of measured mass $m$ kg.

- ★ Temperature of block is taken = $\theta_1$.
- ★ Block is heated for $t$ seconds at a steady voltage ($V$) and steady current ($I$).
- ★ New temperature is taken = $\theta_2$.
- ★ Energy supplied = $VIt$ joules.
- ★ Assuming no heat loss to room:

  Energy received = $VIt$

  $$= m \times c \times (\theta_2 - \theta_1)$$

- ★ $$c = \frac{VIt}{m(\theta_2 - \theta_1)}$$

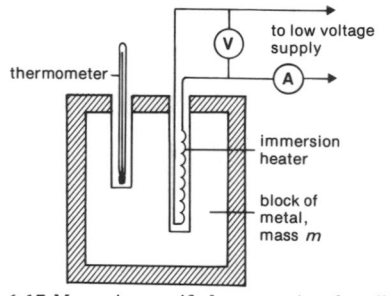

Fig. 6.17 *Measuring specific heat capacity of a solid*

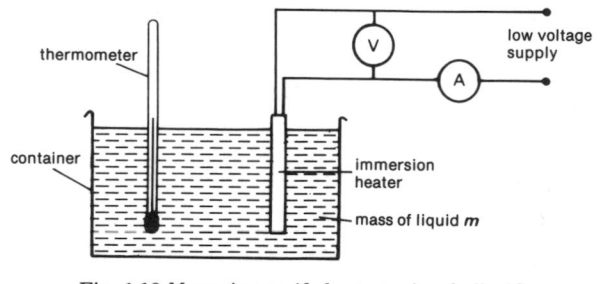

Fig. 6.18 *Measuring specific heat capacity of a liquid*

2  For a **liquid** (see Fig. 6.18).
   ★ Electric immersion heater placed in liquid of mass $m$ kg.
   ★ Liquid is heated and temperatures taken before and after.
   ★ Same formulae apply.
   ★ This is only an approximate method – for more accuracy you must consider the energy needed to warm the container.

## Change of state and latent heat

Matter exists in three states – solid, liquid and gas. Latent heat is the energy needed or given out when a substance changes its state. For a change from solid to liquid, or from liquid to gas, energy is needed. For a change from gas back to liquid, or from liquid back to solid, energy is given out.

### *Specific latent heats*

1  **Specific latent heat of fusion** is the energy required to change unit mass of substance from its solid state to its liquid state without any rise in temperature. The units are J/kg, e.g. water is 334,000 J/kg.
2  **Specific latent heat of vaporization** is the energy required to change unit mass of substance from its liquid state to its vapour state without any rise in temperature. The units are J/kg, e.g. water is 2,260,000 J/kg at 100 °C.
3  Notice that almost seven times as much energy is needed to change 1 kg of water to steam as for 1 kg of ice to water.
4  The energy required to change the state of a mass $m$ of a substance = mass × specific latent heat, i.e. energy needed = $mL$ joules.
5  This is also the energy given out when the change occurs in the other direction.

### *Melting and freezing*

Melting occurs when the molecules in a solid gain energy and separate enough to weaken their mutual attraction – the molecules become 'free' enough to form a liquid. A *pure* solid substance melts at one particular temperature – its **melting point**. Melting point can be affected by:

1 **pressure** – applying pressure to ice lowers its melting point by a very small amount;
2 **impurities** – adding salt to melting ice can lower its melting point to −18 °C.

## Boiling
A liquid boils when its molecules have sufficient energy to escape from all parts of the liquid. **Boiling point** is affected by:
1 **atmospheric pressure** – increased pressure raises the boiling point, e.g. in a pressure cooker; reduced pressure lowers it;
2 **impurities** raise the boiling point of a liquid, e.g. salt in water.

## Evaporation
1 A liquid **evaporates** when it changes to a gas at a temperature below its boiling point.
2 Evaporation takes place only at the surface of a liquid.
3 It occurs because some molecules in a liquid move faster than others.
   * The 'energetic' ones escape from the liquid surface.
   * The remainder of the liquid is cooled – cooling by evaporation.
4 Rate of evaporation is affected by:
   * temperature difference between liquid and surroundings – the greater the difference the greater the evaporation;
   * area of liquid exposed – the greater the surface area the greater the evaporation;
   * rate of removal of vapour above liquid – if it is blown away the evaporation rate increases;
   * amount of vapour present in air – if air is saturated, evaporation will not occur;
   * volatile liquids evaporate more readily – their molecules need less energy to escape; a drop of ether on your hand evaporates quickly, cooling it as it takes up heat for evaporation.

### Cooling by evaporation

1 The human body has its own cooling system – perspiration evaporates from the body surface, energy needed being taken from the body itself, which cools down.

2 Refrigerators are cooled by evaporation of a volatile liquid, e.g. Freon.

   ★ Freon evaporates inside freezing compartment.
   ★ Energy for evaporation is taken from the freezing compartment, cooling it.
   ★ Freon condenses outside the fridge, giving out energy.
   ★ This energy warms the air near the fridge.

# 7   ELECTRICITY AND MAGNETISM

## Electrostatics

### *Electricity and matter*

1   Some materials **conduct** electricity, others are **insulators**.
   ★ Metals are good conductors of electricity, copper and silver being amongst the best.
   ★ Solutions of acids and salts are good liquid conductors.
   ★ Gases are generally very poor conductors although under certain extremes of high electrical potential and reduced gas pressure they can conduct.

2   All matter is made of atoms, which consist of three **elementary particles**:
   ★ **protons** – have a positive electric charge $(+)$;
   ★ **neutrons** – have no electric charge;
   ★ **electrons** – have a negative electric charge $(-)$ equal and opposite to the charge on a proton.

3   The bulk of the atom is made up protons and neutrons (**nucleons**) packed tightly together in a central nucleus. The electrons orbit the nucleus. The number of protons in an atom is equal to the number of electrons (the atom is electrically neutral).

4   Electrons, particularly those in outer orbits, can become detached – the ease with which this happens determines to what degreee a material can act as a conductor or insulator of electricity.

5   Electrons are more easily removed by electrical, chemical and mechanical forces than are the other particles because:
   ★ mass of electron is approximately 2,000 times less than mass of a neutron or proton;
   ★ forces holding neutrons and protons in the nucleus are very much greater, and of a different nature, than those between nucleus and electrons.

6   An **electric current** is a movement of electrons, measured in amperes (A).

7   The unit of **electric charge** (quantity of electricity) is the coulomb (C).

8   1 ampere = 1 coulomb/second.
9   The smallest quantity of electricity is $1.6 \times 10^{-19}$C (charge on
    one electron); thus:

$$1A = \frac{1}{1.6 \times 10^{-19}} = 6 \times 10^{18} \text{ electrons/second}$$

## Conductors and insulators

1   **Metal conductors** have relatively large numbers of free or
    easily freed electrons which can drift from atom to atom. An
    organized drift due to an applied electric potential is an
    electric current.
2   **Liquid conductors** are electrolytes. The carriers of the elec-
    tric current are ions.
3   In **gas conductors** the carriers of electric current are both
    ions and electrons. At very high temperatures a gas becomes a
    plasma – atoms are stripped of electrons leaving ions and
    electrons.
4   **Insulators** (non-metals) have electrons firmly held in their
    orbits, so the electrons cannot move.
5   **Semiconductors** conduct some electricity.
    ★ Not as good as metals – they have fewer available
      electrons.
    ★ Charge carriers may be positive, negative or both.

## Static electricity

1   If two insulators of electricity are rubbed together and separ-
    ated, some electrons from one insulator can be pulled to the
    other – electrification by friction, or **static electricity**.
2   If an insulator has an **excess** of electrons on it as a result of the
    friction it has a **negative** charge; a deficiency of electrons
    produces a **positive** charge.
    ★ No charge is detected unless the two materials are separ-
      ated, since the net electric charge is zero.
    ★ There are only two types of charge, positive and negative.
    ★ The charges on the two insulators are equal and opposite.
3   For electric charges to remain on any material the material
    must be either an:

* **insulator** – few free electrons are available to sustain an electric current; charge produced at any point on its surface will remain in that region;
* **insulated conductor** – the charge will be distributed over its surface; electric potential will be the same at all points; density of distribution of charge is dependent upon shape of conductor, can be found using a proof plane and an electroscope; at a **point**, charge may be so concentrated that it leaks away as an 'electric wind' (action of points is used by lightning conductors to lower charge on a thundercloud).

### *Like and unlike charges*

1 Two identical insulating materials rubbed with the same cloth, e.g. ebonite rods rubbed with fur, will oppose each other when brought together – they have been given identical negative charges (see Fig. 7.1).

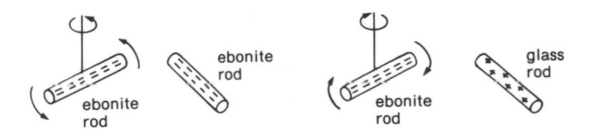

Fig. 7.1 *(a) Like charges repel. (b) Unlike charges attract*

2 A glass rod rubbed in silk (or cellulose acetate rod rubbed in wool) and brought near the ebonite rod will be attracted since the glass or cellulose has been given a positive charge.
3 Like charges repel each other; unlike charges attract each other (as in magnetism).
4 When a body acquires a charge, there is an electric field in the space around the body and the body acquires an electric potential. Whether a body has a positive or negative potential depends upon zero standard (reference point) – the earth is considered at zero potential.

### The leaf electroscope

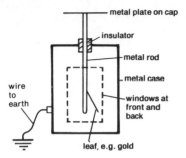

Fig. 7.2 *Leaf electroscope*

The divergence (opening) of the leaf depends on the potential difference between it and the case when a charged body is brought near.

1 **Detecting charge** – a positively charged body is brought near to an uncharged electroscope.
   * Free electrons are attracted to the cap.
   * The leaf and rod, both having a positive charge, repel and the leaf diverges (see Fig. 7.3).

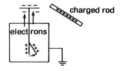

Fig. 7.3 *Detecting charge*

2 **Charging electroscope by contact** – a charged body touches the cap of the electroscope, giving cap a charge of same sign (on contact electrons move freely between charged body, cap

and gold leaf). When body is removed there is a potential difference between leaf and case, indicated by leaf position.

3 **Charging electroscope by induction** (see Fig. 7.4).

- ★ To charge electroscope positively a negatively charged rod is brought near the cap – leaf opens.
- ★ Cap is momentarily earthed and electrons move to earth – leaf closes.
- ★ Keeping rod near cap, the earth connection is removed.
- ★ Rod is removed and leaf opens – it has a positive charge.
- ★ Electroscope is negatively charged if positively charged rod is used.

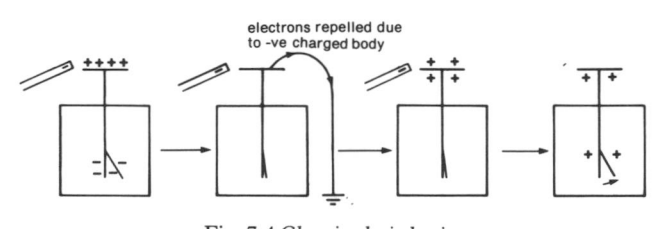

Fig. 7.4 *Charging by induction*

4 **Finding the sign of a charged body.**
- ★ Electroscope is charged positively or negatively using a known charged body.
- ★ Body of unknown sign is brought slowly up to the cap.
- ★ If leaf closes, the body could have a sign opposite to that of the leaf *or* it could be uncharged.
- ★ Only true identification is if leaf continues to open when the body is brought closer to the cap.
- ★ In this case the sign on the charged body is the same as that on the cap and gold leaf.

## *Capacitors and capacitance*
1 Potential of a conductor increases when charge on it increases (earth's potential is 0).
2 The ratio of the charge ($Q$) on a conductor to its potential ($V$) is its **capacitance** ($C$):

$$C = \frac{Q}{V}$$

where $C$ is in farads (F), $Q$ is in coulombs, $V$ is in volts.

3  A **capacitor** stores electric charge.
   *  Consists of two metal plates separated by insulating material.
   *  Charged by connecting it to a battery.
   *  Discharged by removing battery and connecting plates together (see Fig. 7.5).

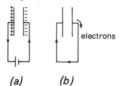

*(a)*        *(b)*

Fig. 7.5 *Parallel plate capacitor. (a) Charge. (b) Discharge*

4  The capacitance of a capacitor depends on:
   *  surface area of plates – the greater the surface area the higher the capacitance;
   *  distance between plates – capacitance increases as plates are brought closer together;
   *  insulating material between plates – **dielectric**.
5  Dielectric is used to:
   *  keep the plates apart;
   *  raise capacitance;
   *  reduce the chance of electrical discharge, enabling large differences to be used – the higher the potential difference, the higher the charge stored.

## Cells and batteries

1  **Cells** convert chemical energy into electrical energy.
2  Two or more cells connected together form a **battery**.
3  A **primary** cell cannot be re-charged; a **secondary** cell can be.

### The simple cell

1  Two plates, one of copper, one of zinc, are placed in dilute sulphuric acid (see Fig. 7.6).
2  If the two plates are connected by a conductor, external to the cell, then:
   *  bubbles of hydrogen gas form at the copper plate;
   *  there is a flow of electrons through the conductor from zinc to copper.

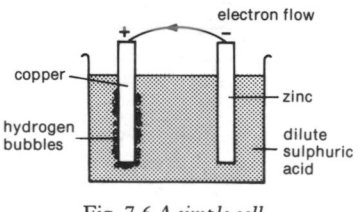

Fig. 7.6 *A simple cell*

3  The electromotive force (EMF) of a cell is equal to the potential difference (in volts) across its terminals when it is not producing current in a circuit – the total energy transformed (joules) per coulomb of electric charge passing in a circuit in which the cell is connected. A simple cell has an EMF of about 1V.

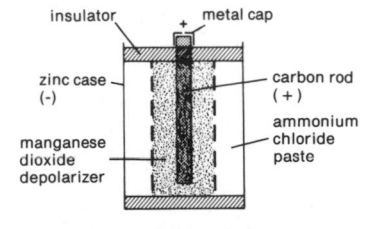

Fig. 7.7 *A dry (Leclanché) cell*

### The dry cell
This has an EMF of 1.5V. It is used in torch and radio batteries, but has a limited life (see Fig. 7.7).

### The lead–acid cell (accumulator)
This can be re-charged. It has an EMF of 2V (see Fig. 7.8).

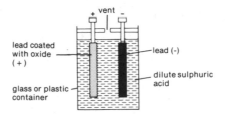

Fig. 7.8 *Lead–acid cell (accumulator)*

### PD and EMF
1 **PD** and **EMF** are *not* the same.
2 For a cell the maximum PD across it can equal the EMF when it is not being used to drive a current through a circuit.
3 If PD across a cell is measured when it is driving a current through a circuit there will be a potential drop across the terminals due to cell's internal resistance.
4 An EMF can exist whether there is a current or not.

### Cells in series and parallel
Cells may be connected to form a battery in two ways.
1 In **series**:
   ★ total EMF is the sum of the EMF of the individual cells;
   ★ the combined internal resistance is equal to the sum of the individual resistances.
2 In **parallel**:
   ★ total EMF is the same as for one cell only;
   ★ the internal resistance is calculated as resistances in parallel are calculated (see page 90).

## Current, voltage and resistance

### *Current*
1  Electric current is a flow of charge.
2  Unit of electric current is the **ampere** (A) – that constant current which, if maintained in two infinitely long conductors placed 1 m apart, causes each to exert a force of $2 \times 10^{-7}$ N/m on the other.
3  Unit of electric charge is the **coulomb** (C) – the charge passing any point when a current of 1 A lasts for 1 second.
   Charge=Current×Time, i.e. $Q=It$, $I=Q/t$
4  In metals, current is flow of electrons. Electron flow is in the *opposite* direction to conventional current (see Fig. 7.9).

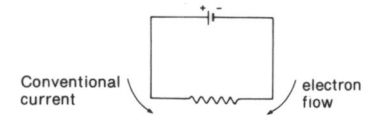

Conventional current

electron flow

Fig. 7.9 *Conventional current and electron flow*

5  Use the conventional current direction for all rules, laws, etc., but be aware that electrons flow from negative to positive.

### *Voltage*
1  Potential difference (PD) is energy transformed (joules) when a charge of 1 C is moved from one point to another.
   Energy=PD×Charge
   $W=V\times Q$
2  PD is measured in **volts** – the PD between two points if 1 J of energy is transformed when 1 C moves between these two points.

### *Ohm's law*

**Ohm's law** – current passing through a wire (metallic conductor) at constant temperature is proportional to the potential difference applied between its ends. It can be verified as follows.

1  Set up the circuit shown in Fig. 7.10.

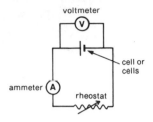

Fig. 7.10 *Ohm's law experiment*

2  Set the rheostat at a suitable value. Do *not* adjust it while values are taken.
3  Note the readings on the ammeter and voltmeter.
4  Add a second identical cell in series connection and re-read the ammeter and voltmeter.
5  Repeat, adding a further cell each time.
6  The ratio $V/I$ should be a constant ($k$) over a limited range.
7  Graph of $V$ (volts) plotted against $I$ (amps) produces a straight line passing through the origin, i.e. $V \propto I$.

## *Resistance*

1  An electrical supply connected across the ends of a metallic conductor will produce a current dependent on the electrical resistance of the conductor.
2  Resistance ($R$)   $\dfrac{\text{PD across the conductor } (I)}{\text{Current through conductor } (I)}$

where $R$ is in ohms, $V$ in volts and $I$ in amps, i.e.
$R = V/I$ or $V = IR$
3  Providing temperature remains constant, devices that have a constant resistance are called **ohmic** conductors.
4  Non-linear conductors do not have a constant resistance with PD/current variation, e.g. semiconductors, diode valves, thermistors, electrolytes, photoresistors.

### Resistors in series and parallel

1 Resistors connected in **series** – total value of resistance in a circuit ($R_T$) is equal to the sum of the individual values of resistance (see Fig. 7.11).

$$R_T = r_1 + r_2 + r_3$$

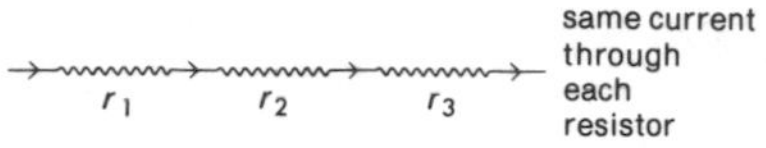

> same current
> through
> each
> resistor

$$\xrightarrow{\phantom{x}} \underset{r_1}{\wedge\!\wedge\!\wedge} \xrightarrow{\phantom{x}} \underset{r_2}{\wedge\!\wedge\!\wedge} \xrightarrow{\phantom{x}} \underset{r_3}{\wedge\!\wedge\!\wedge} \xrightarrow{\phantom{x}}$$

Fig. 7.11 *Resistances in series. Total resistance* $= r_1 + r_2 + r_3$

2 Resistors connected in **parallel** (see Fig. 7.12)—total value of resistance in a circuit ($R_T$) can be found by:

$$\frac{1}{R_T} = \frac{1}{r_1} + \frac{1}{r_2} + \frac{1}{r_3}$$

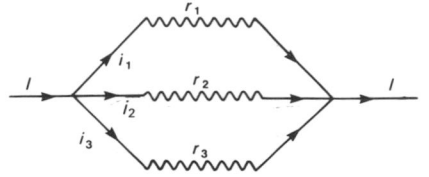

Fig. 7.12 *Resistances in parallel, same PD across each resistance,*
$I = i_1 + i_2 + i_3$

3 At the junction of the three resistors connected in parallel, the circuit current ($I$) splits into three values ($i_1, i_2, i_3$) such that $I = i_1 + i_2 + i_3$. The current values depend upon the resistance values – larger resistance, smaller current.

### Measuring resistance

1 A suitable circuit containing the unknown resistor ($R$) is set up (see Fig. 7.13).
2 With the rheostat set at a suitable value, readings of ammeter and voltmeter are taken.

**3** Rheostat is varied and new values of PD and current are taken.

**4** Procedure repeated for several rheostat settings.

**5** Resistance ($R$) determined either by:
* averaging the values of resistance;
* plotting a graph of $V$ against $I$ – gradient equals $R$.

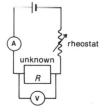

Fig. 7.13 *Measuring an unknown resistance*

## Measuring the internal resistance of a cell

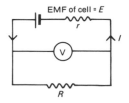

Fig. 7.14 *Measuring internal resistance*

**1** A cell has known EMF ($E$) and unknown **internal resistance** ($r$).

**2** The cell is placed in a circuit with a known resistance ($R$):
$$E = I(R+r)$$
where $R+r$ is the total circuit resistance.

91

3  A voltmeter is connected across $R$ and PD measured (see Fig. 7.14):
$$V = IR$$
for the resistance $R$.
4  $V$ is less than $E$.
5  The 'lost' volts drive current through internal resistance of cell:

'Lost' voltage $= \text{EMF} - \text{PD}$

$$E - V = (I(R+r)) - IR$$
$$= Ir$$

6  Current through cell is the same as current through resistor:

$$I_{\text{cell}} = \frac{E - V}{r}$$

$$I_{\text{resistor}} = \frac{V}{R}$$

$$r = \frac{(E-V)R}{V}$$

### *Resistivity of a material*

The resistance of a wire depends on:
1  its length $(l)$;
2  its cross-section area $(A)$;
3  the material it is made of.

To compare materials we use their **resistivities**:

Resistance of a wire $(R) = \dfrac{\rho l}{A}$

where $\rho$ is the resistivity of material in ohm-metres.

### *Temperature and resistance*

1  The resistance of most metals **increases** with temperature.
2  Semiconductors, e.g. silicon, germanium, become better conductors as they get warmer, i.e. their resistance **decreases** with temperature (also true of carbon).
3  **Thermistors** are made of semiconductor material – their resistance decreases as they get warmer.

# The effects of an electric current

## The heating effect

1 Energy is expended in maintaining an electric current in a circuit.
   * When electrons pass through a conductor part of their energy is converted to thermal energy.
   * The temperature rises as they collide with the atoms of the conductor.

2 Energy transformed by an electric current $(W)=$ PD×charge:
$$W=V\times Q$$

3 $Q=It$

4 Thus:
$$W=VIt \text{ (in joules)}$$

5 But as:
$$V=IR$$
we have:
$$W=I^2Rt=\frac{V^2t}{R}$$

6 Power supplied by electric current is energy supplied per second:
$$\text{Power }(P)=\frac{\text{Energy supplied}}{\text{Time taken}}\text{(in watts)}$$
$$=IV=I^2R=\frac{V^2}{R}$$

7 The **kilowatt-hour** (kWh) is the unit of energy used on electricity bills.
   * It is energy supplied if 1,000 watts are used for an hour.
   * 1 watt=1 joule/second, therefore $1\,kWh=1,000\times 60\times 60=3,600,000$ joules.

## Uses of the heating effect

1 Heating element of **electric fire** is made of resistance wire, the temperature of which is raised to about 900°C when connected to the mains.

2 Resistance of electric **light bulb filament** is chosen so that when connected to AC mains supply it glows white hot.

(Prevented from oxidizing by enclosing it inside a glass envelope containing inert gas at low pressure.)

3   To prevent overloading, **fuses** are inserted into electrical circuits – fuse wire melts, breaking circuit, when current exceeds certain value.

4   **Hot wire ammeter** indicates current in a wire by detecting expansion in length as temperature of wire rises.

### The chemical effect

1   A liquid that conducts electricity and is at the same time decomposed is an **electrolyte**.

2   The process by which chemical decomposition occurs as a result of the passage of a current is **electrolysis**.

3   Two electrodes, the **anode** (+) and **cathode** (−), connect the solution to positive and negative terminals of the battery.

4   Electricity in electrolytes is carried by ions – atoms or groups or atoms which have lost or gained one or more electrons.

### The magnetic effect

A wire carrying an electric current produces a magnetic field.

This can be detected by placing a compass needle close to the wire (see next section).

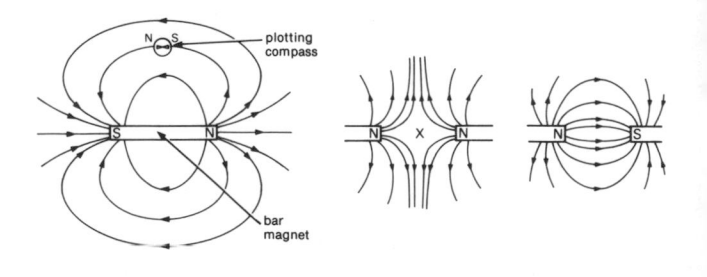

Fig. 7.15 (a) Magnetic field around bar magnet. (b) Repulsion (X = neutral point). (c) Attraction

# Magnetism

## *Magnetic fields*

1 A **magnetic field** is a region of magnetic influence surrounding a magnet.
2 Any ferromagnetic material in this region is influenced by it.
3 A magnetic field is represented by **lines of force** – lines along which a free north pole would move.
4 Magnetic field patterns can be detected by:
   * **iron filings**;
   * a small plotting **compass**
5 Magnetic lines of force *never* cross.
6 Magnetic forces are most concentrated at the ends (**poles**) of a magnet.
7 If a north pole of a magnet is brought near the north pole of another magnet, **repulsion** occurs.
8 If a north pole of a magnet is brought near a south pole of another magnet, **attraction** occurs.
9 **Like poles repel, unlike poles attract**
10 Positions of no magnetic influence (**neutral points**) occur where the resultant field is zero.

## *Magnetizing and demagnetizing*

Magnetic materials are materials that can be made into magnets, e.g. iron, cobalt, nickel, alloys containing these elements. 'Soft' materials can be used for **electromagnetics**; 'hard' materials can be used for **permanent** magnets.

1 A *hard* magnetic material can be magnetized by:
   * stroking with another magnet;
   * placing a bar inside a long coil (**solenoid**) and passing a large direct current through the coil for a second.
2 Materials can be **demagnetized** by:
   * heating strongly;
   * hammering;
   * dropping repeatedly;
   * withdrawing slowly from inside a solenoid carrying a large alternating current.

## Magnetic fields due to an electric current

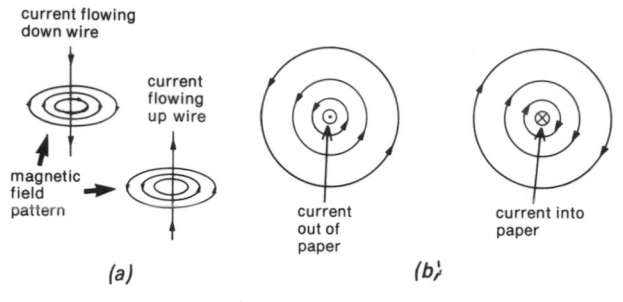

Fig. 7.16 *Field around current-carrying wire (a) from the side (b) from above*

1 Magnetic field around a current-carrying **wire** can be found by **Maxwell's corkscrew rule**. Imagine a right-handed screw being turned so that it moves along the wire in the same direction as the current – direction of turning shows direction of magnetic field (see Fig. 7.16).

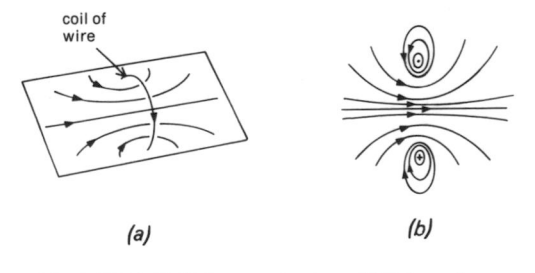

Fig. 7.17 *(a) Field due to a circular coil (b) from above*

2 Magnetic field pattern due to a circular **coil** is shown in Fig. 7.17. The strength of the field may be increased by:

* increasing the current;
* increasing the number of wires, or turns;
* reducing the radius of the coil.

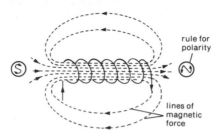

Fig. 7.18 *Field due to a solenoid*

3   Magnetic field due to a **solenoid** is shown in Fig. 7.18. The polarity rule predicts poles at each end of the solenoid. Viewing one end of the coil, it will have:
    * north pole if current is in anticlockwise direction;
    * south pole if current is in clockwise direction.

The strength of the field can be increased by:
    * increasing the current;
    * increasing the number of turns;
    * placing a soft iron rod inside solenoid (an **electromagnet**).

### Uses of electromagnets
1   The **electric bell** (see Fig. 7.19).
    * When push switch is pressed, current is set up in circuit.
    * Soft iron formers become electromagnets and attract soft iron connected to striker.
    * Striker hits the bell.
    * As striker hits bell, contact point at screw is broken and current ceases in circuit.
    * Soft iron formers no longer act as electromagnets and release soft iron striker which returns to the screw.

★ Circuit is now remade and process is repeated until push switch is released.

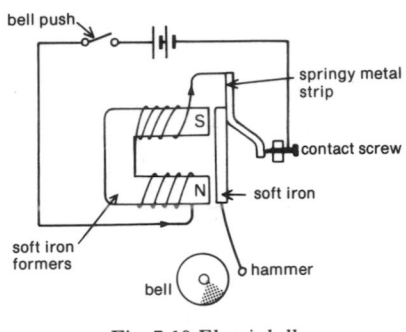

Fig. 7.19 *Electric bell*

2 **Magnetic relay** – a switch operated by an electromagnet, used in telephone exchanges, car starter-motor circuits.
3 **Telephone earpiece** – vibrating diaphragm is pulled by an electromagnet inside the earpiece; the vibrations produce sound waves.

## Meters and motors: the motor effect

### *The motor effect*
A wire carrying an electric current, placed at right angles to a magnetic field, experiences a force, the direction of which can be predicted by **Fleming's left-hand rule** (see Fig. 7.20).
1 Thumb, first and second fingers of the left hand are placed at 90° to each other.
2 First finger indicates direction of magnetic field (N→S).
3 Second finger indicates direction of current.
4 Thumb indicates direction of force acting on wire (motion).
The force is caused by the interaction of two magnetic fields – the field around the current-carrying wire and the field due to the magnet itself. If the wire is free to move, it will move in the

direction of the force. This effect is used in moving-coil galvanometers, electric motors, moving-coil loudspeakers.

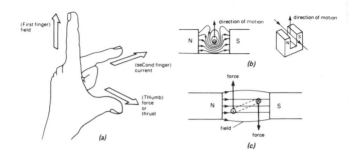

Fig. 7.20 (a) Fleming's left-hand rule. (b) Single force. (c) A couple

### Galvanometers
The most sensitive form of moving-coil meter, the galvanometer (see Fig. 7.21) is the basis of many instruments used to measure current and PD. It consists of a rectangular coil of wire carrying a pointer suspended in a magnetic field produced by two opposite poles of a strong magnet.

1 When a current passes through the coil via the suspensions it experiences a couple which rotates it about its centre in a direction predicted by Fleming's left-hand rule.
2 Opposing this rotation is a hairspring which applies a restoring couple.

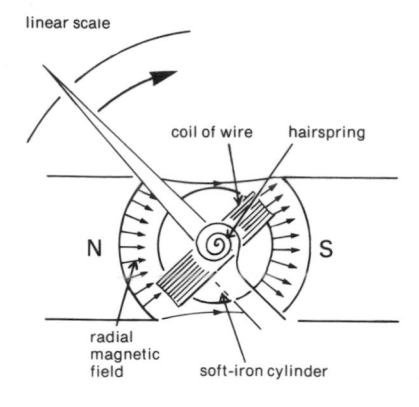

Fig. 7.21 *Moving coil galvanometer*

**3** When the two couples are equal and opposite, the pointer is
set in a steady position.
**4** Increasing the current in the coil increases the magnitude of
the magnetic couple – the pointer is pushed further over until
the coiling of the spring again produces a couple which
equally opposes the magnetic couple.
**5** The further the pointer of a meter moves for a given circuit
the more **sensitive** the meter. The sensitivity can be increased
by:
  ⋆ using a stronger magnet;
  ⋆ using a weaker hairspring;
  ⋆ making the pointer longer;
  ⋆ increasing the number of turns on the coil.
**6** **Full-scale deflection** of a galvanometer is the current needed
to make the pointer move the full distance of the scale – 15
milliamps (mA) is a typical value.

### Converting a galvanometer to an ammeter

A galvanometer can be used with much larger currents, e.g. up to 10 amps, by connecting a low resistance **shunt** across its terminals, i.e. in parallel.

**Example:** A meter with a full-scale deflection of 15 mA is converted to measure a current of 10 amps maximum. Fig. 7.23 shows how most of the current ($I$) is diverted through the shunt.

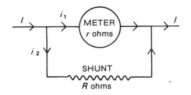

Fig. 7.22 *Using a shunt*

1 For a full scale deflection the maximum current taken by the meter is 15 mA (0.015 A).
2 $I = i_2 + i_2$. If $I = 10$ amps, 9.985 amps must be shunted through the resistor ($R$).
3 Since PD across both meter and shunt is the same (they are in parallel), PD across meter = PD across shunt.
4 $V = IR$ for meter and shunt.
5 Therefore $i_1 r$ (for meter) $= i_2 R$ (for shunt), i.e.
   $0.015 \times 10 = 9.985 \times R$.
6 The shunt resistance ($R$) has a value of 0.015 ohms.

### Converting a galvanometer to a voltmeter

A high resistance bobbin (**multiplier**) enables a meter to measure large voltages. The multiplier is connected in series.

**Example:** A meter is used to measure a maximum PD of 1,000 V. For a full-scale deflection the maximum PD needed is only 0.15 V (see Fig. 7.23).

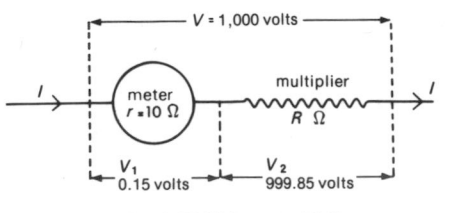

Fig. 7.23 *Using a multiplier*

1  The potential drop across any bobbin must be 999.85 volts, since $V = V_1 + V_2$.
2  The current through both meter and bobbin is 0.015 A for a full scale reading on the galvanometer.
3  $V = IR$ for bobbin.
4  Therefore $R = \dfrac{V}{I} = \dfrac{999.85}{0.015} = 66{,}657$ ohms.

### The direct current (DC) electric motor

1  A rectangular coil of wire, mounted on a spindle and placed horizontally in a magnetic field, experiences a couple, causing it to rotate, if a current is passed through it.
2  The coil continues to rotate until it is perpendicular to the field direction. At this position no couple is experienced by the coil (check using Fleming's left-hand rule).
3  The current given to the coil has to be reversed at every half-turn if the coil is to continue rotating in the same direction.
   *  This reversal is achieved by a **commutator** split in two parts that connect with opposite ends of the coil.
   *  As the commutator rotates with the coil, electrical contact occurs with two carbon **brushes** which press on the commutator sections.
4  The coil's motion will take it past the vertical position even though at that point it is *not* receiving a couple due to the motor effect.

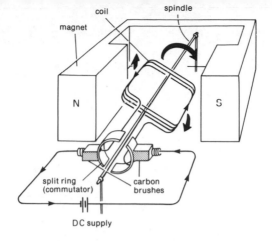

Fig. 7.24 *Simple DC motor*

5  Electric motors have several coils, each with its own pair of
   commutator pieces.
   * This ensures greater turning effect and smoother running.
   * The coils are wound on laminated cores to reduce eddy
     currents set up in the core and to concentrate field
     strength.

## Electromagnetic induction and dynamos

### Laws of electromagnetic induction

If a wire moves through, and cuts, lines of force produced by a
magnetic field, an EMF is induced in the wire – **electromagnetic
induction**. It occurs whenever there is relative movement
between a magnet and a wire. If the wire is part of a complete
circuit, a current is induced. **Fleming's right-hand rule** (see Fig.
7.25) predicts direction of the induced current.

1 Thumb, first and second fingers of the right hand are placed at 90° to each other.
2 First finger indicates direction of magnetic field (N→S).
3 Thumb indicates motion of wire.
4 Second finger indicates direction of induced current.

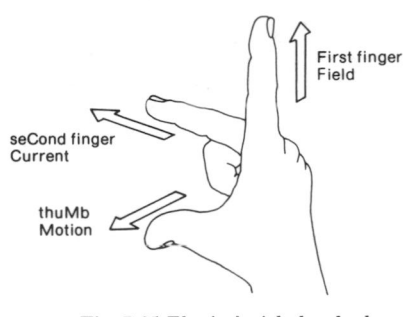

Fig. 7.25 *Fleming's right-hand rule*

There are two laws of electromagnetic induction
1 **Faraday's law** – the strength of the induced EMF is proportional to the rate at which the lines of force are cut. The EMF can be increased by increasing:
   ★ the speed of the motion;
   ★ the strength of the magnetic field;
   ★ the length of conductor cutting the field;
   ★ the number of conductors in series, like the turns of a coil.
2 **Lenz's law** – the direction of the induced current in the wire is always such as to oppose the motion producing it.

### AC generator
1 A rectangular coil of wire is rotated in a magnetic field and a current induced in it.
2 Each end of the wire is connected to a separate slip ring that rotates with the coil.
3 The induced current is conducted away by two spring-loaded brushes (see Fig. 7.26).

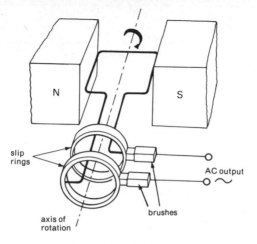

Fig. 7.26 *Simple AC generator*

4  At time $t=0$ induced current $I=0$; coil position is perpendicular to the magnetic field.
5  As the coil rotates clockwise and more lines of force are cut, $I$ increases until, after $\frac{1}{4}$ of a revolution, it is at its maximum.
6  This maximum falls to 0 again during the next $\frac{1}{4}$ cycle.
7  After this $\frac{1}{2}$ revolution the current direction is reversed (check using Fleming's right-hand rule).
8  During the next $\frac{1}{2}$ revolution the current reaches a maximum, falling to 0 again as it completes its cycle – note change of current direction.

A graph of induced current against time for one cycle is shown in Fig. 7.27. The number of revolutions that the coil makes each second is called the frequency of rotation. Frequency of AC mains in the UK is 50 Hz (50 complete cycles/second).

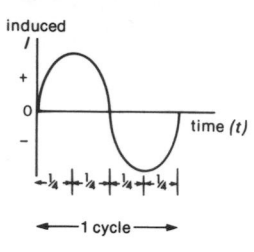

Fig. 7.27 *Alternating current*

## A DC generator

An AC generator can produce DC if the slip rings are replaced by a split-ring commutator, as in the DC motor (see Fig. 7.24). A DC generator is just a DC motor used in reverse.

## Mutual induction and the transformer

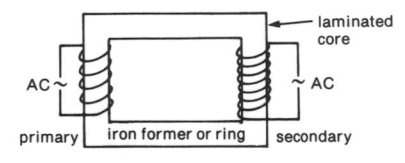

Fig. 7.28 *A transformer*

1 An alternating current in a coil of wire produces a continually varying magnetic field.
2 This varying field can induce a current in a second coil of wire close to it.
3 The effect is **mutual induction** and is used in the transformer (see Fig. 7.28).
4 AC is passed through some primary coils of wire wrapped on one side of a closed iron ring.

5 Continual change of magnetic flux (according to Lenz's law) sets up a current in the secondary coils to oppose it.

6 Current set up in the second coil will alternate to oppose the changing field at all times.

7 If the transformer were 100% efficient:

$$\frac{\text{EMF at the secondary}}{\text{EMF at the primary}} = \frac{\text{No. of coils on secondary}}{\text{No. of coils on primary}}$$

$$\frac{E_s}{E_p} = \frac{n_s}{n_p}$$

8 A step-up transformer is one in which the number of coils on the secondary is greater than the number of coils on the primary – opposite for a step-down transformer.

9 For 100% efficient transformer:

Power input = Power output

Real transformers are never 100% efficient due to heat losses and eddy currents.

### Eddy currents

1 A change in magnetic flux in a conductor induces **eddy currents** which oppose the change of flux – an example of Lenz's law (conservation of energy).

2 Waltenhafen's pendulums demonstrate eddy currents.
   ★ A large solid metal pendulum swung in a magnetic field is quickly brought to rest by eddy currents.
   ★ These currents oppose the motion producing the change in magnetic flux in the pendulum.
   ★ If pendulum is slotted with air gaps, eddy currents cannot circulate – the pendulum is less electromagnetically **damped** so it continues to swing for longer.

3 Eddy currents can be reduced:
   ★ in transformers – soft iron former is laminated with alternate layers of iron strips and insulating shellac, reducing the circulation of eddy currents, making a transformer close to 100% efficient;
   ★ in motors and generators – rotating armature is laminated, reducing eddy currents generated by armature rotating in magnetic field; eddy currents would otherwise slow down rotation.

### Measuring alternating current
1 A **moving-iron ammeter** used to measure AC and DC.
2 Two soft-iron bars, one fixed and one movable, are placed inside a coil.
3 When a current flows in the coil both bars become magnetized in the *same direction*.
4 Movable bar is repelled, moving a pointer across a scale.

## Mains electricity and domestic use

### The national grid
Mains electricity is produced by huge generators in power stations and carried by a national supply network – the **grid**. The grid system uses high voltage trnasmission to reduce power loss. After generation a step-up transformer raises the voltage to 400,000 V for distribution over long distances. At the receiving end it is progressively stepped down to 240 V for use in the home.

**Example:** A cable of resistance 1 ohm is used to transmit 50 kW of power.
1 At 240 V:

$$\text{Current } (I) \text{ in cable} = \frac{\text{Power}}{\text{Voltage}} = \frac{50,000}{240} = 200\,\text{A}$$

Heat loss $= I^2R = 200^2 \times 1 = 40\,\text{kW}$, i.e. almost 80% of generated power is lost in heating the cable.
2 At 40,000 V:

$$\text{Current } (I) = \frac{50,000}{400,000} = 0.12\,\text{A}$$

Heat loss $= I^2R = 0.12^2 \times 1 = 0.01\,\text{W}$ – a greatly reduced power loss.

### Domestic wiring
1 Mains electricity is AC.
2 It comes into a house via:
   * electricity board **main fuse**;
   * **meter**;
   * **consumer unit** ('fuse box').
3 Mains sockets are often connected to a **ring main** (single cable beginning/ending at consumer unit).

4 Ring main protected by 30 A fuse or circuit breaker at consumer unit.
5 Each domestic unit is protected by its own fuse in the plug.

### Three-pin plugs
1 Cable in ring main has three wires:
   * **live**;
   * **neutral**;
   * **earth**.
2 Three wires in flex on a domestic appliance are colour coded:
   * live – **brown**;
   * neutral – **blue**;
   * earth – **yellow** and **green**.
3 **Fuse** values are calculated using power$=V\times I$, e.g. $2\,kW=2,000\,W=240\times I$, i.e. $I=8.3\,A$.
   * Fuse value should be slightly higher than current expected, e.g. 10 A (more commonly 13 A) in this case.
   * If current exceeds fuse value, fuse melts (**blows**) – safety measure.
4 **Earth wire** is another safety measure.
   * It connects metal frame of appliance to earth.
   * If fault develops and live wire touches metal frame, the current flows to earth and blows the fuse.

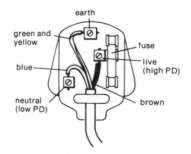

# 8   ATOMIC PHYSICS AND ELECTRONICS

## Electrons

### *Thermionic emission and cathode rays*
Electrons are emitted from a hot metal surface by **thermionic emission** – electrons 'evaporating' from a hot conductor in same way as water molecules evaporate from hot water. Beams of fast-moving electrons are called **cathode rays**. They:
1   excite fluorescence in crystalline salts;
2   travel in straight lines from cathode $(-)$ to anode $(+)$;
3   can be deflected by a magnetic field;
4   can be deflected by an electric field;
5   can pass through thin aluminum foil;
6   carry negative charge;
7   convey energy;
8   have a heating effect when absorbed.

### *Diodes*
Cathode rays *were* used in thermionic diodes ('valves'). **Semiconductor diodes** (silicon, germanium) are now used. Diodes allow current to flow in one direction only. They do *not* obey Ohm's law (see Fig. 8.1).

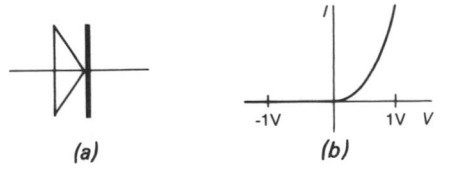

*(a)*                          *(b)*

Fig. 8.1 *(a) Symbol (b) characteristics of a diode*

### *Rectification*
Diodes are also called **rectifiers** (convert AC to DC).
1   Half-wave rectifier is a single diode in series in a circuit. Only half of the AC waveform is used (see Fig. 8.2).

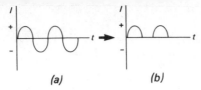

Fig. 8.2 *Half-wave rectification (a) in (b) out*

2 A double diode or two diodes connected 'back-to-back' gives full-wave rectification (see Fig. 8.3).

Fig. 8.3 *Full-wave rectification*

3 Full-wave rectification gives a pulsating DC supply.
   ★ To achieve a steady current a **smoothing circuit** is used.
   ★ The simplest circuit involves a large capacitor in parallel with load (*R* – see Fig. 8.4).

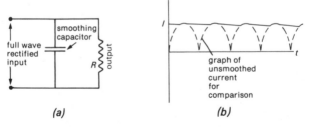

Fig. 8.4 *(a) Smoothing circuit. (b) Output*

**4** A rectifying **diode bridge** (bridge rectifier) with smoothing capacitor produces full-wave rectified AC (see Fig. 8.5).

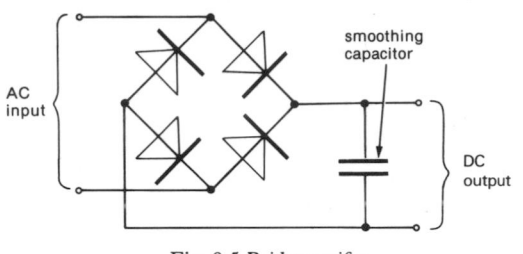

Fig. 8.5 *Bridge rectifier*

*Cathode ray oscilloscope (CRO)*

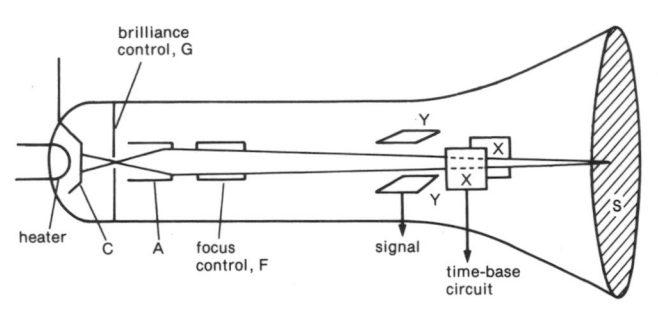

Fig. 8.6 *Cathode ray oscilloscope*

The main parts of a CRO (see Fig. 8.6) are as follows.
**1** **Heater** and **cathode** (C).
**2** **Brilliance control** (G).
**3** **Anode** (A) accelerates and focuses electrons emitted by C.
**4** **Electrode** (F) acts as electron 'lens'.
**5** Pair of **X-plates** deflect electron beam sideways at a rate controlled by the **time-base**.
**6** Test or signal voltage connected to pair of **Y-plates** deflects beam vertically.

**7 Fluorescent screen** (S).

The CRO has many uses, including:

1 studying waveforms, e.g. sound waves – connect microphone across Y-plates;
2 measuring DC or AC voltage – apply it to Y-plates;
3 measuring frequency of waveform – compare pattern on screen with known frequency.

A **TV** is similar to a CRO but its electron beam is deflected by magnetic fields.

## Atomic structure

### Protons, neutrons and electrons

In atoms there is a central nucleus made up of particles – **protons** and **neutrons**. Encircling the nucleus in specific orbits are a third type of particle – **electrons**, e.g. hydrogen (simplest) atom contains one proton around which spins one electron in a spherical orbit. More complex atoms can contain over 90 of each particle type.

1 An atom is about $10^{-10}$ m in diameter.
2 Its nucleus is about $10^{-15}$ m in diameter.
3 Protons have a positive charge.
4 Electrons have a negative charge.
5 Neutrons have no charge.
6 Protons and neutrons have same mass – about $1.7 \times 10^{-27}$ kg.
7 Electrons have about 2,000 times smaller mass than protons and neutrons.

### Atomic number and mass number

1 A **nuclide** is any atom containing a specific number of protons and neutrons.
2 The **atomic number** $(Z)$ of an element is the number of protons in the nucleus.
3 The **mass number** $(A)$ of an atom is the number of nucleons, i.e. the sum of the protons and neutrons.
4 If two atoms have the same atomic number $(Z)$ but a different mass number $(A)$ they are **isotopes** and have the *same* place in the periodic table.

113

5   Any given nuclide is represented by $_Z^A X$, e.g. hydrogen = $_1^1 H$, uranium 238 = $_{92}^{238} U$, isotopes of chlorine = $_{17}^{35} Cl$ and $_{17}^{37} Cl$, isotopes of carbon = $_6^{12} C$ and $_6^{14} C$.

## *Nuclear energy*

1   Nuclear **fission** – a uranium atom split in two by introducing a neutron into its nucleus releases some of its energy as heat.
   ★   About $10^{-11}$ J of energy is released per atom.
   ★   In a **nuclear reactor** the reactions are controlled.
   ★   In an **atomic bomb** they are uncontrolled – a chain reaction.
   ★   Nuclear fission produces dangerous highly-radioactive waste materials.
   ★   The reaction can be shown by an equation:
       $_{92}^{235} U + _0^1 n \longrightarrow _{56}^{144} Ba + _{36}^{90} Kr + _0^1 n + _0^1 n$ + energy, where $_0^1 n$ represents a neutron.

2   Nuclear **fusion** occurs if two light atoms join to form a new atom of higher atomic mass.
   ★   Fusion reaction is the basis of the **hydrogen bomb** (thermonuclear bomb).
   ★   The **sun** also converts mass into energy by this process.
   ★   Typical reaction with heavy hydrogen (deuterium) is:
       $_1^2 H + _1^2 H \longrightarrow _2^3 He + _0^1 n$ + energy
   ★   Nuclear fusion only occurs when the atoms collide at very high speeds and have temperatures of many millions of K.

## Radioactivity
Radioactivity is the emission of rays or particles from the nuclei of certain nuclides. Radiation can be of three types:
1   **alpha** ($\alpha$) particles;
2   **beta** ($\beta$) particles;
3   **gamma** ($\gamma$) rays.

## *Alpha particles*
1   An $\alpha$-particle is a helium nucleus – 2 protons and 2 neutrons.
2   When a nuclide emits an $\alpha$-particle, $A$ decreases by 4 and $Z$ decreases by 2, e.g.:

3 α-particles fluoresce on a phosphor.
4 They are deflected in electric and magnetic fields.
  ⋆ The fields have to be powerful.
  ⋆ The direction of deflection indicates positive charge.
5 Speed of ejection of an α-particle depends on the nature of the emitting nucleus – about $10^7$ m/s.
6 α-particles are stopped by 10–15 mm of air and $10^{-2}$ mm aluminium foil.
7 They affect a photographic plate.

## Beta particles

1 A β-particle is a fast-moving electron.
2 In β-decay, $A$ stays the same and $Z$ increases by 1, e.g.:
   $$^{24}_{11}Na \longrightarrow \, ^{24}_{12}Mg + \, ^{0}_{-1}\beta$$
3 β-particles give less fluorescence on a phosphor than α-particles.
4 They are easily deflected in electric and magnetic fields – direction of deflection indicates negative charge.
5 Speed of a β-particle varies over a wide range; can approach the speed of light.
6 β-particles can travel about 1 m in air and through several mm of aluminium.
7 They affect a photographic plate.

## Gamma-rays

1 γ-rays are electromagnetic waves of very short wavelength.
2 They are not deflected by either electric or magnetic fields.
3 The speed of γ-radiation is the same as for all electromagnetic radiation ($3 \times 10^8$ m/s).
4 γ-rays are stopped by about 90–110 mm of lead, i.e. are very penetrating.
5 They affect photographic plates.
6 γ-emission does not affect mass number or atomic number.

## Half-life

1 The **half-life** of a radioative nuclide is the time taken for half the atoms in a given sample of the substance to decay.

2  Half-lives can vary from $10^9$ years to fraction of a second.
3  The **activity** of a radioactive source is the number of disintegrations per second.
4  The decay curve in Fig. 8.7 shows how the activity of iodine 131 changes with time – the half-life is 8 days.

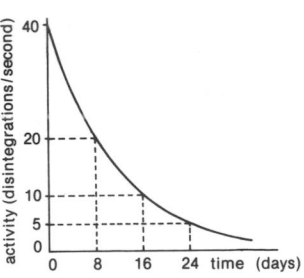

Fig. 8.7 *Decay curve for iodine 131*

## Methods of detection
1  **Photographic plates.**
   * Earliest detectors of radioactivity.
   * $\alpha$- $\beta$- and $\gamma$-radiation all affect photographic emulsions.
2  **Scintillation counters** – $\alpha$-radiation especially can be detected by fluorescence in the phosphor of a scintillation counter.
3  **Ionization.**
   * When radiation passes through matter it can detach electrons from the atoms, leaving **ions**.
   * The detached electrons join other atoms to make negative ions.
   * This is ionization.
   * $\alpha$-radiation is the most ionizing, $\gamma$ the least.
   * A **Geiger–Müller (GM) tube** is a sensitive ionization chamber, used in conjunction with a loudspeaker, scalar or ratemeter to detect radiation. Ions are produced in the gas inside and a pulse of current flows in the circuit. These pulses are counted by a scalar.

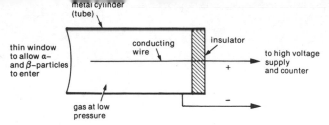

Fig. 8.8 *Geiger–Müller tube*

* In **cloud chambers** charged particles leave a trail of ions
  behind them; this occurs in a region where vapour condenses to liquid; the ions leave a trail of droplets which
  show their path; the nature and energy of the ionizing
  radiation can be determined by observing the traces.
* A **charged leaf electroscope** can be used to detect $\alpha$-radi-
  ation; air near the cap of the electroscope is ionized; ions
  are attracted to the cap, neutralize some of the charge, and
  the leaf falls.

## Uses of radioactivity

1 Radioisotopes are used in medicine, biology and industry as
  **tracers**.
2 In some extreme medical conditions patients are treated by
  exposure to radioactive source.
3 **Archaeological dating** – carbon 14 (radioactive isotope) is
  used to determine the age of very old objects.

Radiation damages living cells in the human body – precautions
must be taken.

1 Short exposure.
2 Screening, e.g. working behind a lead shield.
3 Working at a safe distance, e.g. with forceps.

# Notes